Labyrinths of Truth: Uncovering, Understanding, and Debunking Conspiracy Theories in the Age of Digital Disinformation

From the Secret History of the Illuminati to the Mysteries of the Pandemic: An Essential and In-depth Guide to Navigate the Sea of Fake News, Decode Hidden Messages, and Build Critical Thinking in the Modern Age.

Alex Brown

1. **Introduction** • Definition of "conspiracy theory." • Why are these theories so appealing?

2. **History of Conspiracy Theories** • Historical milestones. • How they have evolved over time.

3. **Definition of the "New World Order"** • Origins of the term. • Different meanings over time.

4. **Means of Dissemination** • The role of traditional media. • The impact of social media.

5. **Popular Conspiracy Theories** • The Illuminati. • Population control. • Ufology and extraterrestrial conspiracies.

6. **Psychological Factors** • Why do people believe in conspiracy theories? • The need to find an enemy.

7. **Impact on Society** • Distrust of institutions. • Influence on political decisions.

8. **The Role of Science and Education** • Controversial conspiracy theories like those

Introduction In a complex and rapidly changing world, where information is increasingly accessible but often distorted, the need for understanding and clarity has never been stronger. It is in this context that conspiracy theories flourish, promising simple explanations to complex questions, even though they are often based on questionable premises.

Definition of "Conspiracy Theory" A "conspiracy theory" can be defined as a belief or explanation that suggests that events or situations are the result of secret, malevolent, and orchestrally planned activities by a powerful group or entity, rather than the outcome of visible, public, or natural causes. In general, these theories assert that what is presented to the public as "truth" is actually a lie, concealed by those who benefit from misinformation.

Why Are These Theories So Appealing?
Conspiracy theories are appealing for a variety of reasons:

1. **Simplification**: In a complex world, these theories offer simple and direct explanations to big and intricate problems. If something goes wrong, it's the fault of a "they," a shadowy and powerful group operating in the background.

2. **Sense of Control**: Accepting that the world is chaotic and unpredictable can be frightening. Believing in a conspiracy theory can give a sense

of having superior insight into events, even if based on false premises.

3. **Affiliation**: Believing in a conspiracy theory can create a sense of belonging. The "aware" become a kind of elite holding a hidden "truth" concealed from the masses.

4. **Confirmation of Beliefs**: These theories often reinforce pre-existing convictions. For example, if someone is distrustful of the government, a theory that claims the government is hiding the truth will be particularly attractive.

5. **Empowerment**: Defending against seemingly omnipotent powers provides a sense of resistance and rebellion.

The Attraction of Conspiracy Theories: An In-Depth Analysis In an attempt to understand the inexhaustible appeal of conspiracy theories, it is essential to delve deep into the psychological, historical, and social roots that give rise to such beliefs. In addition to the previously mentioned factors, there are many other facets contributing to the attraction of these theories.

Historical Origins The need to find culprits or alternative explanations for traumatic or incomprehensible events has deep historical roots. Since ancient times, societies sought explanations for unexpected or catastrophic events. Conspiracies were a way to attribute these events to human causes rather than uncontrollable or divine forces.

Biology of Fear From a biological perspective, humans are programmed to perceive threats. This survival mechanism can make people prone to seeing hidden intentions even when they do not exist. In a modern environment where physical threats are fewer, this predisposition can manifest as a search for "invisible threats," as suggested by conspiracy theories.

Desire for Uniqueness The theory of personal uniqueness suggests that people have an innate need to feel special or unique. Believing in a conspiracy theory can satisfy this need by allowing the individual to possess exclusive knowledge.

Role of Distrust Distrust of authorities or institutions can predispose people to believe in alternative theories. This skepticism may stem from past experiences of deception or corruption by powerful entities.

Confirmation Bias Humans tend to seek, interpret, and remember information in ways that confirm their existing beliefs. This makes people particularly vulnerable to misinformation aligning conspiracy theories with their convictions.

Social Exclusion Individuals who feel marginalized or excluded from society may be particularly inclined to believe in conspiracy theories, as these offer an explanation for why they feel alienated.

Cultural Influence Certain cultures or societies may be more prone to conspiracies due to a history of oppression, colonialism, or injustice. In these contexts, conspiracy theories may seem more plausible because there is a historical precedent of deception by dominant powers.

Narrative and Storytelling Stories are a powerful means through which humans make sense of the world. Conspiracy theories, often presented as compelling narratives of heroes and villains, can be much more attractive than complex or nuanced explanations.

Conclusion The appeal of conspiracy theories is multifaceted and complex. While their prevalence may be concerning, it is essential to understand the motivations behind these beliefs to effectively address them. Through education, awareness, and the promotion of critical thinking, it is possible to hope for countering the rise and attractiveness of these theories in the modern era.

History of Conspiracy Theories Conspiracy theories are not a modern phenomenon; they have existed for centuries, if not millennia. Although specific narratives and details change, the foundations of these suspicions and beliefs have remained constant over time.

Historical Overview

1. **Antiquity**: Even in ancient Rome, conspiracies were commonplace. One of the most famous examples is the Catiline conspiracy, a failed attempt to overthrow the Roman Republic. These real instances of conspiracy fueled paranoia and distrust towards leaders and powerful figures.
2. **Medieval Period**: During the Middle Ages, religious-related conspiracies were particularly prominent. Accusations of heresy and witch hunts were often fueled by conspiracy theories. Jews, in particular, were often falsely accused of plots, such as the infamous "blood libel."
3. **Modern Age**: The French Revolution and the assassination of King Louis XVI gave rise to many theories. Freemasonry and the Illuminati, both esoteric groups, became the focus of numerous conspiracy theories accusing them of seeking to establish a new world order.
4. **20th Century**: The last century witnessed a proliferation of conspiracy theories. The assassination of JFK, the Roswell incident, and the September 11 attacks are just a few examples. The Cold War also brought forth a host of

conspiracies, with both sides accusing each other of espionage and sabotage.

Evolution Over Time

1. **Media Channels**: With the advent of print, radio, television, and, more recently, the internet, conspiracy theories have become more widespread and accessible. The web, in particular, has allowed for the viral spread of these theories.
2. **Social Complexity**: As societies have become more complex, so have conspiracies. For example, while a conspiracy in ancient Rome might involve a handful of senators, a modern theory could implicate entire government agencies or multinational corporations.
3. **Institutional Response**: Initially, conspiracy theories were often seen as a direct threat to power and were suppressed. Today, while some theories are still viewed with suspicion by authorities, others are simply ridiculed or ignored.
4. **Globalization**: In an increasingly interconnected world, conspiracy theories are no longer confined to a single nation or culture. Theories originating in one country can quickly spread and adapt to completely different contexts.
5. **Pseudo-Scientificity**: In the 20th century, many conspiracy theories began to cloak themselves in a veneer of "scientificity," citing

false studies or misinterpretations of research to legitimize their claims.

As we delve into the history of conspiracy theories, it becomes evident how these narratives and tales have played a crucial role in shaping public perception of events. Conspiracy theories often arise in response to traumatic or incomprehensible events. Take, for example, the assassination of Abraham Lincoln: while the assassin, John Wilkes Booth, and his accomplices were swiftly identified and pursued, theories suggesting larger forces at work, government involvement, or hidden motives behind the assassination also emerged. This pattern has repeated on countless occasions. After the death of Princess Diana, despite overwhelming evidence pointing to a tragic accident, theories implicating the British royal family, intelligence services, and other entities arose. The need to find meaning, motive, or a scapegoat behind tragic events is deeply rooted in human psychology. Another factor that has influenced the evolution of conspiracy theories is the dynamics of power and resistance. Often, conspiracy theories emerge as a way for ordinary people to challenge or question official narratives presented by the elite in power. This can be seen as an attempt to rebalance power by giving a voice to the marginalized or the suspicious. Furthermore, conspiracy theories have adapted and mutated with technological innovations. While they were once conveyed through spoken word, books, or letters, today the internet and social media have given these theories unprecedented reach and speed. This has had both advantages and disadvantages. On one hand, it has allowed people to share and discuss these theories in broader communities, providing a platform for collective fact-checking and analysis. On the other hand, it has also facilitated the spread of unverified and false information, making it more challenging to distinguish reality from fiction. It is interesting to note that some conspiracy theories, initially ridiculed or dismissed, have in rare cases been subsequently validated. These rare events have bolstered the credibility of other theories, even if they had no direct basis. For example, revelations about the CIA's MKUltra program, a secret mind control program during the Cold War, lent credibility to many other theories about government manipulation, even if they were not directly related.

The Role of Popular Culture Popular culture has also played a significant role in the evolution and dissemination of conspiracy theories. Movies, books, and television programs dealing with conspiracies, both real and imaginary, have amplified public interest and, in some cases, blurred the line between fiction and reality. This blending of fact and fiction has further complicated efforts to uncover the truth behind many events and phenomena.

The Impact of Multinationals and Global Interconnectedness in the 20th and 21st Century The growing influence of multinational corporations and global interconnectedness in the 20th and 21st century has also opened the door to internationally-reaching conspiracy theories. Organizations such as the UN, the World Bank, or even global corporations have often been at the center of theories accusing them of plotting for global dominance or manipulating economies and governments. These theories reflect people's concerns and insecurities in an increasingly globalized world, where decisions made thousands of miles away can have a direct impact on people's daily lives.

The Intersection of Conspiracy Theories and Politics The interaction between conspiracy theories and politics is another crucial aspect to consider. Throughout history, various political figures, both in power and in opposition, have used these theories as tools to achieve various objectives. Whether to delegitimize opponents or strengthen their own power, conspiracies have become weapons of mass manipulation.

During the Cold War, for example, both the East and the West used conspiracy theories to portray the other as a sinister threat, often associating adversaries with far-reaching plots. Disinformation operations, designed to sow discord or create false alarms, often had conspiracy theories at their core.

In totalitarian or authoritarian regimes, conspiracy theories have frequently been used to justify purges, repression, or even genocides. By creating an invisible and omnipresent enemy, those in power can justify otherwise unjustifiable actions and keep a population in a state of fear and dependence on the government.

Influence on Social and Revolutionary Movements Conspiracy theories have also influenced social and revolutionary movements. At times, these movements arise in response to real perceptions of injustice, but conspiracy theories can exacerbate tensions by providing a simple and monolithic explanation for complex problems. Instead of addressing the nuances and complexity of social, economic, or political issues, people can find comfort in a narrative that clearly identifies "good" and "bad" actors.

The Digital Age and the Spread of Conspiracy Theories With the advent of the digital age, the speed and ease with which conspiracy theories can be created and disseminated have reached unprecedented levels. Online forums, blogs, and social media sites have become self-sustaining ecosystems where theories can be shared, discussed, and amplified without the need for verification or critical scrutiny. This environment, coupled with the "filter bubble" effect – where individuals are primarily exposed to information that reinforces their pre-existing beliefs – has created a situation where conspiracy theories can thrive and radicalize without opposition.

The Economic Aspect Another noteworthy aspect is the role of conspiracy theories in the economy. Some individuals have found that fueling or promoting these theories can be lucrative. This can occur through the sale of books, monetization of videos on platforms like YouTube, or even through the sale of products promising protection from alleged conspiratorial threats.

The Power of Belonging The power of conspiracy theories also lies in their ability to provide a sense of belonging. In a world that can seem chaotic or incomprehensible, believing in a conspiracy theory can offer a sense of order and purpose. It also provides a community of like-minded believers, a group that shares a hidden "truth" withheld from the masses. This sense of belonging and superiority can be deeply enticing, especially in times of uncertainty or change.

Balancing Skepticism and Open-Mindedness Finally, while many conspiracy theories are unfounded, there is always the danger of automatically dismissing any suggestion of a conspiracy as pure fantasy. Historically, there have been real conspiracies that were initially ridiculed or rejected, only to later be revealed as true. The challenge, then, is to strike a balance between healthy skepticism and an open mind, recognizing that in a complex world, not everything is always as it seems.

The History of Conspiracy Theories The history of conspiracy theories is intrinsically intertwined with the history of humanity itself. These theories have emerged and developed in response to our deepest needs to make sense of the world, find order in chaos, and assign meaning to often incomprehensible or traumatic events. These psychological needs have been fueled and amplified by the dynamics of power, politics, and culture, becoming more complex with the advent of new technologies and the information age.

Over the years, we have seen how conspiracy theories have influenced not only individual perceptions but also significant historical events, shaping policies, sparking revolutions, and shaping the course of history. The interplay between reality and fiction, truth and misinformation, has blurred the lines of demarcation, continually pushing society to challenge its own beliefs and question accepted narratives.

The digital age has accelerated the spread of conspiracy theories, democratizing access to information but also complicating the task of distinguishing fact from fiction. In an era where every individual has the capacity to become a content broadcaster, the responsibility for verification and discernment often falls on the individual, making it imperative to educate the masses on critical thinking and media literacy.

Economics, psychology, culture, and technology are all factors that play a role in perpetuating conspiracy theories. But amid all this, a crucial point emerges: while many conspiracy theories can be easily debunked with concrete evidence, it is essential to maintain an open mind and not dismiss every theory as irrelevant or ridiculous. History has shown us that, in rare but significant cases, what may seem like a conspiracy could actually have a basis in truth.

In conclusion, conspiracy theories are a complex and layered phenomenon, rooted in deep human needs and fueled by a myriad of external factors. Understanding their origins, evolution, and impact is essential not only to navigate today's complex information landscape but also to build a more informed, resilient, and cohesive society.

2. History of Conspiracy Theories

• Historical Overview: Conspiracy theories are not a modern phenomenon. They have deep roots in human history, manifesting in various forms and contexts throughout the centuries.

• Antiquity: Conspiracies can be traced back to antiquity. For example, in ancient times, certain natural events were believed to be the result of plots by the gods. The assassination of Julius Caesar is another ancient example of a conspiracy theory, with many speculations about the real motivations and possible masterminds behind the act.

• Middle Ages: In the Middle Ages, conspiracy theories often revolved around religion and power. Accusations of witchcraft or heresy, for example, were often rooted in conspiratorial beliefs. Additionally, accusations against Jews, such as poisoning wells, are another example of conspiracies from this period.

• Modern Era: With the Enlightenment and the rise of the printing press, conspiracy theories began to spread more widely. The French Revolution, for instance, was accompanied by numerous theories regarding both internal and external plots.

• Evolution Over Time: Over time, conspiracy theories have undergone transformation, both in their nature and in the way they are disseminated.

• Technological Innovation: With the advent of the printing press and later mass media such as radio, television, and the Internet, conspiracy theories found new channels for dissemination. The internet, in particular, accelerated the speed at which these ideas can spread, giving them a global reach.

• Social Complexity: As societies became more complex, conspiracy theories also became more intricate. For example, in the 20th century, with events like the assassination of JFK or the September 11 attacks, conspiracy theories became intertwined with geopolitics, espionage, and international power dynamics.

• Pop Culture: In the 20th and 21st centuries, conspiracy theories have also become a cultural element. Movies, books, and television programs have often dealt with these themes, sometimes further fueling speculations. • Reaction to Crises: Conspiracy theories tend to flourish in times of crisis or uncertainty. The COVID-19 pandemic, for example, generated a series of conspiracy theories regarding the origin of the virus, vaccines, and lockdown measures.

Regenerate Over the centuries, as conspiracy theories have adapted and mutated, the core remains: the human need to find answers, often in obscure or hidden places, in an attempt to make sense of the world around us.

The fabric of conspiracy theories is strongly tied to the cultural and sociopolitical nuances of different historical epochs. If we take, for example, the period of the Reformation in Europe, conspiracy theories circulated widely among Catholics and Protestants, each accusing the other of nefarious plots to control the masses and manipulate religious doctrine.

In the colonial era, European powers exploring and colonizing new lands were often viewed with suspicion by indigenous peoples and other European nations. Conspiracy theories regarding the true nature of their missions, secret plans to subdue peoples and territories, and competitions for resources thrived. With the expansion of the British Empire, for instance, many believed there was a hidden plan to dominate the world. These conspiracy ideas were not entirely unfounded, given the vast territory the Empire was accumulating, but they were often exaggerated and based on fears rather than concrete facts.

In the 19th century, with the Industrial Revolution, new conspiracy theories emerged. The radical change brought about by mechanization and urbanization gave rise to concerns about the loss of autonomy and control. These concerns fueled theories about possible manipulation by industrial barons or financial elites. Stories of secret societies, such as the Illuminati or the Masons, operating behind the scenes to control economies and governments, became particularly popular.

The 20th century then saw an explosion of conspiracy theories related to the Cold War. Hostility between East and West fueled numerous tales of espionage, sabotage, and infiltration. It was believed that each superpower was secretly working to undermine the other, and paranoia was palpable. This period also saw the emergence of theories regarding UFO sightings and encounters with extraterrestrials, often linked to alleged government cover-ups.

With the decline of the Cold War and the rise of globalization, conspiracy theories began to focus on international organizations like the United Nations or the Bilderberg Group. Some argue that these entities are working to create a one-world government, while others see conspiracies in attempts to control global resources or manipulate economic events.

The advent of digital technology has offered an unprecedented platform for the spread and amplification of conspiracy theories. The ability to share information in real-time and connect with like-minded individuals worldwide has given voice to many theories, some of which were previously confined to extremely niche circles. Disinformation, fake news, and information manipulation have reached unprecedented levels, making it increasingly difficult for the average individual to distinguish between fact and fiction.

In the 21st century, we have seen an increase in conspiracy theories related to climate change, biotechnology, and scientific innovations. The rapid progress in these fields has led many to speculate about the true intentions behind such advancements. At the same time, the emergence of global pandemics like COVID-19 has brought conspiracy theories regarding the creation of laboratory-made viruses or pharmaceutical plots to the forefront.

The interplay between historical events, technological developments, and human psychological needs has ensured that conspiracy theories remain a constant, albeit ever-changing, part of human history. While circumstances and specific details may change, the tendency to seek hidden patterns, secret agents, and dark forces behind global events persists. And while conspiracy theories can often be easily debunked, their persistence in the fabric of society reflects deep insecurities, fears, and desires to understand an ever-evolving world.

In addition to what has already been discussed, it is interesting to note how conspiracy theories have manifested in different cultures and regions of the world, showing a mix of universal themes and specific local concerns. While in the West, one might cite the Illuminati or conspiracies surrounding the deaths of personalities like Marilyn Monroe, in other parts of the world, conspiracy theories have a distinct local shade.

In the Middle East, for example, conspiracy theories often revolve around regional conflicts, foreign interventions, and religious tensions. You might find those who firmly believe that there are behind-the-scenes plots orchestrated by Western powers to control oil resources or manipulate regional politics. Revolutions and coups often fuel these theories as the population seeks to make sense of tumultuous and often tragic events.

In Asia, conspiracy theories may center around themes such as regional supremacy, territorial conflicts, and the spread of soft power. For example, tensions between India and China have given rise to various theories, as have issues related to the South China Sea. Additionally, Japan's cultural and technological influence during the 20th century, followed by its economic rise and fall, has sparked numerous speculations and conspiracy narratives.

In Africa, conspiracy theories are often linked to post-colonial ties, natural resources like diamonds or rare earth elements, and rapid political changes. Foreign powers' interference, the expansion of multinational corporations, and human rights issues fuel such theories. The continent has a complex history of external interference, exploitation, and resistance, providing fertile ground for the birth of conspiracy theories.

Latin America, with its revolutions, coups, and a history of foreign interference, particularly by the United States during the Cold War, has a rich tradition of conspiracy theories. Operation Condor, a secret operation among various South American governments to combat communist insurgency, is just one example of how reality can sometimes surpass fiction. Furthermore, figures like Che Guevara, Fidel Castro, and many other Latin American leaders are often the focus of conspiracy theories seeking to decipher the true motives behind their actions and deaths.

In the modern era, global interconnectedness and the spread of communication technologies have allowed for a fusion of conspiracy theories from different parts of the world. This global mix has given rise to even more complex and intricate narratives. Theories that were once confined to a particular region now find resonance thousands of kilometers away. This phenomenon has amplified the reach and impact of such theories, creating common ground for people from various cultural and geographical backgrounds. Furthermore, the intersection of these theories with popular culture has further blurred the line between reality and fiction. With cinema, literature, and TV series often drawing from real conspiracy theories to create gripping plots, it has become increasingly challenging for the public to discern where reality ends and fantasy begins. This intricate interweaving has led to further dissemination and acceptance of these theories in societies that might otherwise have been skeptical.

Lastly, the role of social media platforms cannot be ignored. With algorithms designed to maximize engagement, echo chambers are often created, where people are primarily exposed to information that reinforces their pre-existing beliefs and fears. In such an environment, conspiracy theories can flourish undisturbed, fueling divisions and mistrust in institutions and established truths.

3. Definition of the "New World Order" The term "New World Order" (NWO) has had various meanings over the years and can refer to both real political and geopolitical developments and popular conspiracy theories. Here is a detailed definition:

New World Order (NWO) *Geopolitical Definition:* In a historical and geopolitical context, the term "New World Order" has been used to describe fundamental changes in political power and international relations. It is often evoked during periods of great global change or upheaval.

- *Post-World War I:* The use of the term can be traced to the post-World War I era when nations sought to create a new balance of power and prevent future conflicts. This desire manifested in the establishment of the League of Nations.
- *Post-World War II:* The term was again used in the post-World War II period, especially by figures like Winston Churchill. The "New World Order" of that time was characterized by the birth of the United Nations, the division of the

world into Eastern and Western blocs during the Cold War, and the decolonization of Africa and Asia.

- *End of the Cold War:* In the 1990s, following the collapse of the Soviet Union, the term was once more invoked to describe a unipolar world dominated by the United States, with the rise of new economic powers like China and India.

Conspiracy Theories: On the other hand, in conspiracy theories, the "New World Order" often refers to an alleged secret plan orchestrated by global elites to establish a unified world government that would have total control over all aspects of human life. These theories are often linked to themes such as:

- **Global Control:** The idea that a small group of powerful elites is working behind the scenes to establish a single world government.
- **Symbolism:** Supporters of these theories often cite symbols such as the all-seeing eye or the pyramid as evidence of these secret plans. These symbols are seen on banknotes, buildings, and other places, interpreted as manifestations of the hidden influence of the NWO.
- **Organizations:** Entities like the United Nations, the International Monetary Fund, the Bilderberg Group, the Masons, and the Rothschilds are often cited as instruments or protagonists of this alleged conspiracy.
- **Global Events:** Every major crisis or international event, such as wars, financial crises,

or pandemics, is seen by some as steps toward the establishment of this world order.

It should be emphasized that while geopolitical dynamics are a legitimate field of study based on facts and historical analysis, conspiracy theories about the New World Order are often based on speculation, misconceptions, and misinformation. The understanding of the term "New World Order," therefore, strongly depends on the context in which it is used.

The concept of the "New World Order" is not only rooted in politics and conspiracy theories but also has profound cultural, economic, and social implications. The idea of a radical change in the world order raises concerns about sovereignty, culture, and identity.

From an economic perspective, the rise of globalization has often been associated with the concept of a New World Order. Economic integration, the rise of multinational corporations, and the flow of capital across borders have reduced the power of individual nation-states to fully control their economies. This loss of control has fueled fears and speculations. Some see this as a deliberate plan to centralize economic power, while others view it as a natural evolution of capitalism and technology.

Technology, particularly the advent of the digital age, has played a crucial role in shaping perceptions of the New World Order. The speed at which information can now be shared and disseminated has transformed how people perceive the world around them. The internet has given a voice to many who previously had none, allowing the formation of communities and schools of thought that often challenge traditional narratives. This democratization of information has also opened the door to misinformation and manipulation, creating a fertile environment for the proliferation of conspiracy theories.

Culturally, the idea of a New World Order raises concerns about the homogenization of cultures and the loss of unique cultural identities. In an increasingly interconnected world, there is a concern that dominant cultures may overwhelm and replace smaller cultures, leading to a more uniform but less rich world. This tension between globalization and cultural preservation has fueled many discussions and debates about the future of multiculturalism.

The concept of the New World Order also intersects with other ideologies and movements. For example, environmentalism and concerns about climate change have led some to call for a coordinated global response to environmental issues. This call for international cooperation may, for some, seem like a step toward a world government, further fueling conspiracy theories.

Religions have also played a role in shaping the concept of the New World Order. Some eschatological interpretations of Christianity, Islam, and other religions see the emergence of a world government as a sign of the end times. These religious references have deeply influenced the perception and acceptance of New World Order theories in various communities.

As the world continues to evolve and confront new challenges and opportunities, the idea of a New World Order will continue to be a point of discussion, both as a reflection of real power dynamics in the world and as a lens through which these dynamics are seen and interpreted.

The interaction between the New World Order and people's perception has deep roots in human psychology. Understanding how and why people believe in particular theories can shed light on the persistent nature of the New World Order concept.

Human Need for Understanding and Order: Human need for understanding and order is a focal point. When faced with complex or confusing events, our minds often seek explanations that can provide a sense of order or reason. Conspiracy theories, such as the New World Order, offer these explanations by presenting a framework in which events are not random but rather the result of secret plans orchestrated by powerful figures. This provides a sense of clarity and, for some, a sense of control.

The way information is presented and consumed in the modern era also plays a fundamental role in the spread of New World Order ideas. Social media, in particular, has radically changed the information landscape. Platforms that reward sensationalistic and divisive content can amplify theories like the New World Order.

The design of some platforms encourages echo chambers, where users are continuously exposed to content that reinforces their preexisting beliefs, regardless of the accuracy of such content.

Furthermore, in times of socioeconomic uncertainty, people tend to seek culprits or dark forces that may be manipulating events to their disadvantage. Growing economic inequality, demographic shifts, and rapid technological advancements are all factors that can create anxiety and uncertainty in the population. In this climate, theories suggesting a hidden order behind the chaos can gain traction.

The importance of identity and belonging cannot be overlooked. For many people, believing in theories like the New World Order becomes a fundamental part of their identity. Being part of a community of believers can provide a sense of belonging and understanding. This can further strengthen convictions because challenges or criticisms of such theories are seen not only as attacks on the ideas themselves but also as personal attacks.

Another aspect to consider is the evolution of geopolitics and diplomacy. As nations move toward greater multilateralism and interdependence, decisions are often made in international forums such as the United Nations, the G7, the G20, and other organizations. This shift from traditional nationalism to global solutions for global problems can be interpreted by some as a step toward a "world government," further fueling New World Order theories.

In summary, the concept of the New World Order is an amalgamation of historical realities, geopolitical concerns, psychological fears, and cultural influences. As the world changes and adapts to new challenges, interpretations and perceptions of the New World Order are likely to continue evolving and adjusting accordingly.

The concept of the "New World Order" is often intertwined with themes related to the evolution of power structures and the emergence of new technologies. Every technological innovation, every shift in the balance of power between nations, and every new sociocultural trend can become fertile ground for interpretations and speculations.

If we examine emerging technologies, we can see how artificial intelligence, biotechnology, and the 5G network, for example, have often raised concerns and theories about their connection to a supposed New World Order. Artificial intelligence, with its ability to process and analyze vast amounts of data, could theoretically be used to monitor and influence human behavior on an unprecedented scale. This potential power has led many to speculate about the use of these technologies by elite groups to control the masses.

Similarly, biotechnology, particularly the ability to genetically modify organisms, has raised fears about possible manipulations of humans. Speculations range from the creation of "super soldiers" to genetic manipulation to control or influence people's cognitive or emotional abilities.

The rollout and spread of the 5G network have generated a series of conspiracy theories, some of which suggest that this technology could be used to exert direct or indirect control over the population. These ideas often rely on inaccurate or misleading information, but the essence of such theories is rooted in fear of the unknown and suspicion toward poorly understood new technologies.

Global Economic Structures: Global economic structures are also at the center of discussions about the New World Order. Institutions such as the International Monetary Fund, the World Bank, and the World Economic Forum are seen by some as tools of a global elite aiming to dominate the world economy. The decisions made by these organizations can have a profound impact on the economies of entire nations, and the lack of transparency or understanding of these decision-making processes can fuel further speculation and theories.

The growing interest in cryptocurrencies and blockchain technology offers another example of how new trends can fuel discourse about the New World Order. While some people see cryptocurrencies as a means to escape the control of governments and central banks, others theorize that they could be used by elite groups to create a single global currency, further consolidating control over the global economy.

Finally, we cannot ignore the influence of popular culture in shaping and spreading ideas related to the New World Order. Movies, books, TV series, and music often explore themes of control, manipulation, and hidden power, and these narratives can influence the public's perception of the reality of the world they live in.

As new trends emerge and society continues to evolve, interpretations and speculations about the New World Order will inevitably adapt, reflecting the anxieties and concerns of the era in which we live.

The concept of the "New World Order," in its various forms, represents a complex mosaic of fears, expectations, and interpretations about the future of global society. This concept has deeply rooted itself in the collective imagination, evolving and adapting to new contexts and emerging challenges.

At the heart of such theories is the tension between the individual and structures of power. History has shown that over time, power structures change, evolve, and sometimes consolidate. Whether it's empires expanding or new economic blocs emerging, the dynamic between centralized power and individual or national autonomy has always generated debate and speculation.

In the modern era, the rapid pace of technological innovation has amplified these tensions. Access to information, instant communication, and the ability to influence large segments of the population through digital media have created unprecedented opportunities but also new challenges in terms of privacy, autonomy, and freedom.

The interpretation and response to the concept of the "New World Order" vary widely. For some, it represents an opportunity for a more united and collaborative world, where global challenges can be collectively addressed. For others, it evokes fears of centralized control, the loss of sovereignty, and personal freedoms.

These perceptions are further complicated by the increasingly intricate nature of geopolitics and international diplomacy. In a world where economic, political, and social decisions are often made in international contexts, questions about the nature and origin of such decisions are inevitable. The opacity of some of these global institutions fuels further speculation.

In conclusion, the "New World Order," in its essence, is not so much a concrete reality as it is a lens through which people seek to interpret and make sense of a rapidly changing world. It reflects humanity's anxieties, hopes, and expectations about its future. As such, as the world continues to evolve, discussions and speculations about this concept are likely to persist, offering a window into the complex dynamics between individuals, societies, and structures of power in the 21st century.

1. **Means of Dissemination:** The Role of Traditional Media and the Impact of Social Media.

Means of Dissemination

The spread of conspiracy theories is not a new phenomenon, but the ways in which these theories are communicated and shared have undergone significant evolutions over time. The means through which these ideas are conveyed play a crucial role in determining their reach and influence.

The Role of Traditional Media:

Throughout history, newspapers, magazines, radio, and television have had the power to shape public opinion. Conspiracy theories, when covered by traditional media, can gain apparent legitimacy simply because they are presented on a recognized platform.

- **Amplification:** A sensational story or an intriguing theory can capture the public's attention, prompting the media to give it coverage. This can lead to an amplification effect, where a marginal theory may seem more widespread or accepted than it actually is.

- **Credibility:** Presenting a theory in a traditional media context, especially if it is not adequately contextualized or contradicted, can lend an air of credibility to it.

- **Agenda Setting:** Traditional media has the ability to set the agenda for public discussion. If they choose to focus on a particular theory or topic, they can indirectly influence the importance that the public attributes to that issue.

The Impact of Social Media:

With the advent of social media, the dynamics of information dissemination have undergone a profound transformation. Platforms such as Facebook, Twitter, YouTube, and TikTok have democratized access to information, allowing anyone to share and spread their ideas.

- **Virality:** One of the key features of social media is the ability to make an idea go viral. A conspiracy theory can quickly gain traction and spread to millions of people within hours or days.
- **Echo Chambers:** Social media platforms often use algorithms that show users content similar to what they have already liked or shared. This can create echo chambers, where individuals are primarily exposed to information that reinforces their pre-existing beliefs, reducing exposure to contrasting viewpoints.
- **Unverified Sources:** Unlike traditional media, which usually have editorial teams and fact-

checking processes, social media allows anyone to publish content. This has led to an unprecedented proliferation of fake news, distortions, and unfounded theories.

In summary, while traditional media can confer a kind of "legitimacy signal" to certain theories, social media amplifies and spreads them at an unprecedented rate. This combination has made conspiracy theories more pervasive than ever in our modern society.

The spread of conspiracy theories in both traditional media and social media cannot be understood without considering the cultural and technological changes of recent decades.

In the 1970s and 1980s, before the advent of the internet, conspiracy theories were often confined to small communities, niche publications, and late-night radio broadcasts. The barrier to entry for having a voice in the media was quite high; publishing houses, television broadcasters, and radio stations had control over most of the content that the public consumed.

With the rise of cable television in the 1990s, the media landscape began to diversify. Channels dedicated to niche topics emerged, providing platforms for voices that would have previously struggled to find space in mainstream media. This period saw the emergence of programs that explored mysteries, UFOs, and other alternative theories, bringing these ideas to a much wider audience.

The advent of the internet further revolutionized the spread of information. Online forums, such as those on Usenet, became places where conspiracy theories could be discussed and developed. These virtual spaces allowed people from around the world to share information, regardless of its credibility or accuracy.

However, it was with the birth of social media in the new millennium that the spread of conspiracy theories experienced a true boom. With platforms like Facebook, Twitter, and YouTube, people could not only consume content but also create and share it. This greatly lowered the barrier to entry for sharing information. Theories, regardless of their veracity, could now go viral within hours, reaching millions, if not billions, of people.

Another crucial element in the spread of conspiracy theories on social media is content personalization. The algorithms of many social platforms show users content based on their previous online behaviors. This means that if a user shows interest in a particular conspiracy theory, they are likely to be shown similar content in the future. This continuous reinforcement can solidify beliefs and isolate users from contrasting information.

Furthermore, the nature of social media encourages the formation of communities. While in the past, people who believed in alternative theories might have felt isolated, they can now easily find and interact with thousands of like-minded individuals. These groups can act as echo chambers, where ideas are continually reinforced without being challenged.

Another noteworthy point is the growing distrust in traditional media. Studies have shown that trust in journalism and traditional institutions is declining in many parts of the world. This distrust can push people toward alternative sources of information, which often include conspiracy theories.

The interaction between traditional media and new media in the dissemination of conspiracy theories offers us a fascinating and complex overview of the ever-changing nature of information and its perception in the digital age.

On one hand, traditional media, with their historical authority and professional editorial teams, still hold significant power in defining and shaping dominant narratives. These institutions, often backed by centuries of reputation, can, through careful selection and presentation of news, highlight particular theories or topics, making them central to public discourse. However, this very authority has sometimes led to suspicion from parts of the population, leading to feelings of distrust and accusations of representing "official narratives" rather than objective truths.

**On the other hand, social media and digital platforms have democratized access to and distribution of information like never before. This democratization, while positive in promoting freedom of expression, has also brought with it the rampant spread of disinformation, fake news, and unverified theories. The nature of algorithms designed to maximize interaction and engagement often further amplifies these theories, leading users into a spiral of confirmation bias, isolating them from opposing and challenging views.

But what does all of this mean for modern society? The intersection of these two media worlds has created an information ecosystem where truth is often fluid, subject to interpretation, and, in some cases, manipulation. In such an environment, the ability to exercise critical thinking, to question the source and validity of information, becomes essential.

The human drive to seek patterns, connections, and meaning, especially in times of uncertainty, has always fueled the attraction to conspiracy theories. But in an era characterized by information overload and growing polarization, the need for discernment and an informed, critical citizenship becomes even more crucial. Ultimately, the responsibility falls not only on the media but also on individuals to educate themselves and approach information with a healthy skepticism and a desire for understanding.

5. Popular Conspiracy Theories

Conspiracy theories have always played a role in the collective imagination, offering alternative explanations for events or circumstances that often elude common understanding. Some of these theories have become particularly popular, often thanks to their dissemination through various media. Here is an examination of some of the most well-known and persistent conspiracy theories:

Illuminati: Originally, the Illuminati was a real group founded in 1776 in Bavaria, Germany. It was a secret society with Enlightenment goals, promoting personal freedom and opposition to religious and princely control over people's lives. However, over time, the term "Illuminati" became associated with numerous conspiracy theories, claiming that this secret group had managed to infiltrate various global institutions, gaining invisible control over the world. These theories suggest that the Illuminati is behind various global events, working behind the scenes to establish a "New World Order." Their presence is often associated with hidden symbolism in films, music, and even banknotes.

Population Control: The population control theory argues that elite or governmental groups are trying to control or reduce the world's population through various means. These methods include, but are not limited to, vaccinations, birth control, genetically modified foods, and even induced epidemics. One of the most cited examples in this theory is the United Nations' Agenda 21, which is often misinterpreted as a plan to depopulate the planet, even though it is actually an effort to promote global sustainability.

Ufology and Extraterrestrial Conspiracies:
Perhaps one of the most fascinating and widespread conspiracy theories concerns UFOs and the existence of extraterrestrial life. This theory suggests that governments and institutions have secretly interacted with alien civilizations or covered up evidence of UFO sightings. The 1947 Roswell incident, in which a flying saucer is said to have crashed in New Mexico, is often cited as a prime example of this cover-up. Other theories argue that alien technology has been recovered and used for secret technological developments or that hidden alien bases exist, such as the famous Area 51.

The popularity of these conspiracy theories can be attributed to a combination of factors, including distrust in institutions, the human need to find answers to unresolved questions, and widespread dissemination through various media channels. Despite often lacking concrete evidence, their persistence over time attests to their impact on the collective psyche.

The allure of conspiracy theories, especially those with broad appeal like the Illuminati, population control, and extraterrestrial conspiracies, can be seen as a reflection of collective anxieties, curiosities, and fears. While one might wonder why so many people are drawn to these narratives, the answer may lie in a combination of psychological, historical, and cultural factors.

Take, for example, the Illuminati. The fascination with this theory partly lies in mystery and secrecy. We live in an age where global news is always at our fingertips, and the idea that there are still such deep secrets fuels curiosity. The Illuminati is often depicted as puppet masters manipulating global events, suggesting that behind the complexity and apparent chaos of the modern world, there is a hidden order. This need to find order in chaos can reassure some people by providing an explanation for otherwise incomprehensible events.

On the other hand, the population control theory is deeply rooted in contemporary concerns about overpopulation, limited resources, and government authority. In a world where information about population growth, climate change, and resources is readily available, the fear of a hidden agenda to control or limit population growth is not entirely unfounded in the minds of some. This type of theory can also stem from a profound distrust of institutions, fueled by real scandals and perceptions of corruption.

Finally, the fascination with UFOs and extraterrestrial conspiracies touches deeply on our desire to explore and understand our place in the universe. For centuries, humanity has asked questions about our role and the possibility of other forms of life. With the advent of space technology and the increasing discovery of exoplanets, the idea that we are not alone in the universe no longer seems so remote. Theories like the Roswell incident or the secrecy of Area 51 fuel this curiosity, suggesting that there may have already been interactions between humans and extraterrestrials.

All these theories, though different, share a tendency to challenge official narratives and offer enticing alternatives that address deep-seated questions or latent fears. Their spread is further fueled by the viral nature of modern media, where controversial or mysterious stories can quickly gain traction. Moreover, the ability to communicate and share ideas in online communities has provided a platform for these theories to flourish and dynamically evolve.

The human need to seek meaning and order in incomprehensible phenomena has always manifested throughout history. Conspiracy theories offer a narrative that often fills gaps in knowledge by attributing events or situations to hidden and powerful forces operating behind the scenes. While some of these theories are easily debunked with concrete evidence, their adaptability and mutation make them particularly resistant to criticism.

Consider, for example, the persistence of the belief in the Illuminati. Although they were originally an 18th-century society with well-defined goals, their legend has continued to evolve and adapt to contemporary concerns. In the 20th century, with increasing globalization and the intertwining of economies and politics, the Illuminati became the ideal scapegoat for those who believe in a globalist cabal seeking to dominate the world. Popular culture has also played a role in amplifying this myth: movies, books, and music have incorporated the image of the Illuminati, often attributing to them exaggerated powers and intentions.

Population control theories strike a particular nerve, especially in an era where biotechnology and medicine are advancing by leaps and bounds. The ability to manipulate the human genome, create vaccines, and influence biology at the molecular level has led many to fear that these technologies could be used in ethically questionable ways. Additionally, with increasing urbanization and population density in many areas, the idea of deliberate population control is not entirely foreign to the fears of many.

As for ufology, the vastness of the universe and the idea that there may be civilizations beyond Earth have always fascinated humanity. Every time an unidentified flying object is sighted, hope and curiosity are renewed that we may not be alone. This theory has gained further traction with access to platforms like

YouTube, where videos of alleged sightings can be shared and viewed by millions of people. Area 51, with its aura of secrecy, has fueled further speculation, with many believing that it houses alien technology or even captured extraterrestrials.

Another crucial aspect in the persistence of these theories is the complexity of the modern world. In an age where information is abundant but often contradictory, many people feel overwhelmed and seek simple explanations for complex problems. Conspiracy theories, however intricate, often offer a linear and unequivocal narrative in which "the villains" are clearly identifiable and responsible for the world's injustices. This type of storytelling can be comforting as it provides a sense of clarity amid chaos.

Furthermore, the polarized nature of politics and media in many societies has contributed to the creation of echo chambers where people are exposed only to information that reinforces their pre-existing beliefs. This phenomenon, known as "confirmation bias," is particularly evident in conspiracy theories. When people are immersed in these echo chambers, it becomes difficult for them to accept or even consider alternative viewpoints.

The pervasiveness and longevity of conspiracy theories in human history, especially in our modern era, cannot be separated from the intrinsic mechanisms of human psychology and the complexity of our information environment. The desire to understand, to find patterns, and to assign meaning to phenomena drives us towards narratives that often offer alternative, if not controversial, explanations for global events.

Conspiracy theories, such as those about the Illuminati, population control, or ufology, provide people with a form of cognitive control. In a world that can seem chaotic or beyond individual control, believing that there is a hidden design or dark forces at work provides a sense of order. For some, it is more comforting to believe in a conspiracy than to accept the arbitrariness or randomness of events.

The growth and proliferation of digital media have played an ambivalent role in the spread of conspiracy theories. On one hand, they have democratized access to information, allowing anyone to share their opinions and seek alternative truths. On the other hand, they have also created information bubbles, where people are exposed only to information that reinforces their preexisting beliefs. This, combined with confirmation bias, has made many conspiracy theories almost impervious to criticism or challenge.

In conclusion, conspiracy theories are not just a passing fad or a deviation from the ordinary understanding of events. Rather, they are the product of deep cultural, psychological, and historical forces.

Their presence and resilience in public discourse should be understood not only as a challenge to accurate information but also as a reflection of human anxieties, hopes, and fears in navigating an increasingly complex and interconnected world. Their ongoing evolution and adaptation to new circumstances and media demonstrate the flexibility and resilience of these narratives, which are likely to continue shaping public and private discourse for a long time to come.

Psychological Factors Why Do People Believe in Conspiracy Theories? Understanding the appeal of conspiracy theories requires a deep look into the intricacies of the human mind. Several psychological factors, often rooted in our evolution as a species, make us susceptible to such beliefs, even when they are contradicted by obvious objective facts. Examining these factors not only helps explain the popularity of such theories but can also offer a path to addressing the spread of misinformation.

Why Do People Believe in Conspiracy Theories?

1. **Need for Meaning and Control:** One of the primary psychological drivers pushing people toward conspiracy theories is the innate need to find meaning in events and to feel a sense of control over the surrounding world. In a seemingly chaotic universe, the idea that there is a hidden design or dark forces at work can offer a degree of comfort. Even if the forces are malevolent, the mere concept of an underlying

order can be preferable to the idea of a purposeless universe.

2. **Confirmation Bias:** People naturally tend to seek, interpret, and remember information in ways that confirm their preexisting beliefs or hypotheses. Conspiracy theories thrive in this environment, offering explanations that align with the worldviews of those who seek them.

3. **Sense of Specialness:** Believing in a conspiracy theory can give people the sensation of possessing secret or special knowledge that the "herd" does not have. This sense of superiority can further reinforce belief in and adherence to such theories.

The Need to Find an Enemy

1. **Simplifying Complexity:** The modern world is complex and often challenging to comprehend. Attributing global challenges, such as economic crises or natural disasters, to a specific group or enemy provides a simplified explanation. This not only makes events more understandable but also offers a clear point of blame.

2. **Group Cohesion:** From an evolutionary perspective, identifying an "external enemy" may have strengthened group cohesion. This may be particularly true in times of uncertainty or crisis, where group solidarity can offer greater security. Conspiracy theories, by identifying a common enemy, can thus serve to strengthen bonds within a community.

3. **Anxiety and Fear Management:** In a world where threats can seem omnipresent but often

intangible (such as climate change, financial crises, or pandemics), having a tangible and identifiable enemy can help people focus on and better manage their anxieties.

In summary, conspiracy theories and the need to find an enemy are deeply rooted in human psychology and history. They offer simplified explanations and a sense of control in a complex world, and they can strengthen group bonds while providing comfort in the face of uncertainty. While some conspiracy theories are easily debunked, their appeal persists due to these psychological factors. Understanding these factors can help address the spread of conspiracy theories and misinformation.

In summary, conspiracy theories and the need to identify enemies are closely tied to fundamental psychological needs of human beings. These needs, though rooted in mechanisms of evolutionary survival, can manifest in ways that challenge logic and reason in the modern era. Understanding these factors can provide a pathway to addressing misinformation and promoting a more critical understanding of global events.

The vast landscape of human psychology, combined with the environment in which we live, creates a complex web of factors that influence our tendency to believe in conspiracy theories. When considering humanity's evolutionary history, we can identify a series of deeply ingrained psychological elements that drive such beliefs.

Fear of the Unknown has been a constant in human history. Faced with dangers like predators or rival tribes, humans have developed a tendency to be hyper-vigilant and to seek patterns. This pattern-seeking, while once advantageous in protecting us from real threats, can now lead us to see connections where none exist, driving the formation and belief in conspiracy theories.

The Need for Belonging to a community has led humans to seek tribes or groups of belonging. In the modern era, this can translate into a tendency to form groups around shared beliefs, including the sharing of conspiracy theories as a way to strengthen community bonds and define who is part of "our" tribe and who is an outsider.

Cognitive Desirability is another crucial factor. People tend to believe what they wish were true, regardless of objective evidence. If a conspiracy theory aligns with a person's aspirations, fears, or resentments, they are more likely to adopt it.

Additionally, in a world where information overload is the norm, many people feel inundated by a constant stream of news and data. In such circumstances, conspiracy theories can offer a kind of "cognitive shortcut," providing simple and direct explanations for otherwise complex events.

Identity Defense also plays a role. People are more likely to believe in conspiracy theories that protect or reinforce their identity, especially if they feel that their identity is under attack. For example, if a person strongly identifies with a certain political group, they may be more inclined to believe in conspiracy theories that cast political opponents in a negative light.

Finally, there's an aspect of **rebellion against authority**. Distrust in traditional institutions, which may be fueled by real events eroding public trust, can lead people to seek alternative explanations to those provided by official sources. This distrust can manifest as a tendency to believe that such institutions are part of larger conspiracies.

In short, the human psyche and its interaction with the surrounding environment provide fertile ground for the proliferation of conspiracy theories. As society evolves, and technology changes the way we interact with information and each other, new factors are likely to emerge that influence this dynamic.

Interest in and trust in conspiracy theories are not the product of irrational or ignorant minds, as is sometimes suggested. Rather, they are the result of a complex combination of psychological, sociological, and evolutionary factors that have shaped human behavior and thinking for millennia. Our predisposition to seek patterns, our need for community belonging, the desire to confirm our preexisting beliefs, the need to simplify an increasingly complex world, and the natural tendency to defend our identity are all deeply rooted drives that can lead us toward conspiracy theories.

The modern information overload, along with a growing distrust in traditional institutions and sources of information, has further amplified these tendencies. In a world where false or misleading news can spread like wildfire through social media, many people find themselves facing a deluge of information without the necessary skills to discern fact from fiction. This can lead to a greater inclination toward theories that, even if unsupported by concrete evidence, appear to offer clarity and confirm preexisting worldviews.

Yet, as we understand the underlying factors of belief in conspiracy theories, it also becomes evident that addressing the phenomenon is not a simple matter. It's not just about educating people with "real facts" but addressing the underlying psychological and social needs that drive such beliefs. Only through a holistic approach that combines education, understanding, and empathy can we hope to counter the growing tide of misinformation and conspiracy theories in the modern world.

7. Impact on Society • Distrust in Institutions • Influence on Political Decisions

Impact on Society Conspiracy theories are not merely products of popular culture or marginal topics of online debate. They have a tangible and often pervasive impact on society at large. To fully understand this impact, it is crucial to examine how these theories affect trust in institutions and political decisions.

Distrust in Institutions:

1. **Erosion of Trust:** One of the major
    consequences of conspiracy theories is the
    erosion of trust in both public and private
    institutions. When people believe that these
    entities are involved in secretive or malicious
    activities, they can become suspicious of
    everything they represent, from official messages
    to proposed initiatives.

2. **Rejection of Science and Expertise:** In an
    era where science and technology play a crucial
    role in society, distrust in institutions can lead to
    a rejection of knowledge and professional
    expertise. This is particularly evident in the
    context of vaccines, climate change, and other
    significant scientific issues.

3. **Undermining Democratic Institutions:**
    Trust is a cornerstone of functioning
    democracies. Distrust in institutions, such as
    electoral agencies or the media, can undermine
    confidence in the democratic process itself,
    leading to a erosion of civic participation and
    social tensions.

Influence on Political Decisions:

1. **Political Mobilization:** Conspiracy theories
    can serve as catalysts for political mobilization. If

a group of people strongly believes there is a conspiracy against them, they may unite to fight it, directly influencing politics at local, national, or international levels.

2. **Policy Formation Based on Fear:** Political decisions can be made based on conspiracy theories rather than concrete evidence or objective analysis. This can lead to ineffective or harmful policies that fail to address real societal challenges.

3. **Polarization:** Conspiracy theories can exacerbate political polarization. When opposing groups adhere to different, often incompatible, narratives about how the world works, common ground shrinks, making constructive dialogue or compromise difficult.

4. Conspiracy theories, as they spread like vast webs of hypotheses and conjectures, not only undermine individual trust but also alter the entire social fabric. Rooted in the depths of the collective psyche, these theories can proliferate and manifest in ways that are sometimes subtle and other times blatant.

5. Looking at institutions, for example, healthcare has been a frequent target of conspiracy theories, especially in the modern era. Consider the widespread idea that cures or remedies for

certain diseases are intentionally concealed from the public to ensure profits for pharmaceutical companies. This perception not only fuels distrust in doctors and researchers but can also lead people to avoid life-saving treatments or turn to untested alternative remedies.

6. The field of education is not immune either. The notion that there is a "hidden curriculum" or that educational choices are made to promote a certain world order can undermine the effectiveness of education itself. Teachers may come under scrutiny, and educational institutions may be viewed with suspicion, compromising the overall value and integrity of the education system.

7. In the political landscape, conspiracy theories can alter perceptions of international relations. The idea that certain nations operate in the shadows to destabilize others, or that international organizations have secret agendas, can lead to distorted foreign policies and decisions based more on unfounded fears than realistic analysis.

8. Furthermore, in the realms of industry and finance, ideas about secret cartels or corporations controlling the global flow of money can lead to

excessive regulations or, conversely, a lack of oversight where it is genuinely needed.

9. Popular culture, including films, books, and television programs, often amplifies these theories, giving them a wider platform. While in some cases this may lead to increased awareness and constructive debate, it often serves only to further spread misinformation.

10. In terms of interpersonal relationships, conspiracy theories can create divisions. Friendships and family bonds can be tested when one person strongly believes in a conspiracy theory and another does not. These divisions can extend to entire communities, creating environments where suspicion and paranoia are the norm rather than the exception.

11. All of these effects, when combined, can have a profound and lasting impact on society. From widespread distrust in institutions and leaders to community and relational divisions, the shadow of conspiracy theories extends far beyond mere gossip or niche theories.

The Use and Impact of Conspiracy Theories in Contemporary Society The use and influence of conspiracy theories in contemporary society are not phenomena to be taken lightly. These belief systems, often rooted in deep-seated fears and misunderstandings, possess a unique ability to alter the perception of reality, erode the fundamental trust that holds our society together, and have tangible repercussions on individual and collective decisions.

Systemic Distrust of Institutions Systemic distrust of institutions resulting from these theories is not merely a passing emotion or isolated phenomenon. It represents a corrosion of trust that can weaken the very foundations upon which our democratic societies are built. When people begin to doubt institutions—whether governmental, educational, healthcare, or media—social cohesion and stability can be endangered. Collective consensus, which enables societies to function smoothly, is compromised.

Influence on Political Decisions Political decisions influenced by conspiracy theories can have far-reaching effects, often in unforeseen or unintended directions. Politics based on fear or suspicion can lead to repressive laws, restrictions on civil liberties, or aggressive foreign policies. What is even more concerning is that when leaders themselves subscribe to such theories, decisions may be made without critical evaluation or a genuine understanding of the implications.

Interconnection with Popular Culture and Modern Media The interconnection of these theories with popular culture and modern media has further amplified their reach. In an era where information can be shared and amplified in an instant, misinformation can spread like wildfire, and previously marginal theories can quickly become mainstream.

Understanding the Vocal Minority However, it is essential to understand that despite the apparent dominance of these theories in certain environments, they often represent the opinions and beliefs of a vocal minority. The challenge for modern societies is not so much to combat each individual theory but rather to educate the masses to think critically, evaluate information sources, and build collective resilience against disinformation.

In Conclusion In conclusion, the rise and persistence of conspiracy theories represent a fundamental challenge for contemporary society. Addressing this challenge will require concerted efforts by educators, leaders, media, and citizens to ensure that truth and trust can prevail over suspicion and doubt. The fabric of society depends on our ability to navigate these turbulent waters with discernment and integrity.

8. The Role of Science and Education Science and education have always been bulwarks against ignorance and superstition. In a world where information is abundant but often misleading, their importance cannot be underestimated. However, despite advances and discoveries, science and education often find themselves in conflict with conspiracy theories.

Controversial Conspiracy Theories such as Vaccine-related Ones A prominent example of this conflict is represented by controversial conspiracy theories related to vaccines. Medical research has repeatedly demonstrated that vaccines are safe and one of the most effective methods for preventing serious diseases. However, for decades, some individuals have claimed that vaccines cause autism or other medical conditions, despite no scientific evidence supporting such claims. These conspiracy theories about vaccines not only jeopardize individual health but also compromise herd immunity, putting entire communities at risk.

The Way These Theories Gain Traction The way these theories gain traction, despite a mountain of contrary scientific evidence, is a clear example of how emotions, distrust, and misinformation can override logic and common sense. Many people, guided by fear or skepticism toward institutions, seek confirmation of their beliefs rather than objectively informing themselves.

The Importance of Critical Education This is where the crucial importance of critical education comes into play. Education should not only transmit information but also teach people how to think, not what to think. Critical education teaches individuals to evaluate information, distinguish between reliable and unreliable sources, and develop logical and rational thinking.

The Role of the Scientific Method For example, the scientific method is not just a set of procedures; it's also a mental approach. It teaches people to ask questions, seek evidence, and be willing to change their opinions in light of new information. This type of critical thinking is the most effective antidote against conspiracy theories.

Effective Critical Education However, for critical education to be effective, it must be integrated throughout the curriculum, from early childhood education to higher education. Additionally, education must extend beyond the classroom. The media, community leaders, and families all have a role to play in encouraging critical and rational thinking.

In Conclusion In conclusion, while conspiracy theories may seem persuasive and enticing, science and critical education provide the tools to see beyond illusions and identify the truth. In an era of misinformation and distrust, promoting education and science is more important than ever to ensure an informed and resilient society.

The Interaction of Science, Education, and Conspiracy Theories The interaction between science, education, and conspiracy theories is deeply intertwined and reflects the tension between knowledge and disbelief that has existed for centuries. In the past, during the Renaissance, for example, scientific progress was often viewed with suspicion and considered heretical. To some extent, this mirrors what is happening today, where some scientific discoveries are viewed with skepticism or even rejected by certain segments of society.

The Advancement of Technology and Information Access The advancement of technology has allowed unprecedented access to information. While this openness has its advantages, it has also created fertile ground for the spread of unverified or misleading information. People are bombarded with information from all directions, making it increasingly difficult to distinguish facts from fiction. In this sea of information, conspiracy theories thrive, fueled by a combination of distrust in traditional institutions and the human tendency to seek patterns and connections, even when none exist.

Challenges Beyond Vaccines The issue of vaccines, as previously mentioned, is just the tip of the iceberg. There are many other areas where science is in conflict with unsupported popular theories. Take, for example, claims about climate change. Despite overwhelming scientific consensus regarding the impact of human activity on climate change, there are still individuals and groups who reject these conclusions as part of a hidden agenda.

Lifelong Critical Education as a Solution Critical education, as a solution to this problem, extends beyond formal schooling. It is essential that people are exposed to critical thinking at every stage of their lives. This entails ongoing training, workshops, and programs that constantly challenge individuals to examine and reevaluate their beliefs.

Role of Universities and Research Institutions Universities and research institutions have a crucial role to play in this. They should actively engage in public outreach, bringing science to people in ways that are both understandable and engaging. This can include everything from public seminars and conferences to podcasts and educational videos.

Media and Scientific Institutions Partnership Furthermore, scientific institutions should work closely with the media to ensure that scientific information is presented accurately and without distortion. This partnership is vital, as the media plays a significant role in shaping public opinion.

Perhaps one of the most crucial keys to countering the spread of conspiracy theories is the creation of a culture in which error and changing one's mind are seen not as signs of weakness but as integral parts of the learning and growth process. If people are not afraid to admit they may have been wrong or to change their minds in light of new information, they may be less inclined to cling to false beliefs even in the face of overwhelming evidence.

The dialectic between science, education, and conspiracy theories represents one of the most intriguing facets of the modern era. It is a tangible manifestation of the struggle between empirically validated knowledge and the human need to find meaning, order, and, in some cases, simple answers to complex questions.

Science, at its core, is an ongoing quest for truth. It relies on the scientific method, which encourages observation, experimentation, and peer-to-peer review to ensure the accuracy of information. However, precisely because of this ever-evolving nature, it may appear ambiguous or uncertain to the general public. When new data emerges, scientific theories can be adapted or modified, but this adaptability is often misinterpreted as uncertainty rather than as an adaptive approach to understanding.

On the other hand, education is the means through which scientific knowledge is transmitted to the masses. But education, to be effective, cannot be limited to a one-way transfer of information. It must promote critical thinking, analysis, and the ability to question and evaluate information. Education should not only teach what to think but how to think.

Meanwhile, conspiracy theories offer seductive and often oversimplified explanations to complex problems. They thrive on ambiguity and distrust, and in today's climate of media saturation and polarization, they find fertile ground to grow and spread.

Therefore, the real antidote to conspiracy theories is not just strengthening science or expanding education, but rather cultivating a culture of curiosity, open-mindedness, and critical understanding. A society that values and respects empirical research, that teaches its members to think critically, and that promotes the understanding and acceptance of the evolution of knowledge is a society resilient to the snares of conspiracy theories.

In conclusion, in an age where "fake news" and misinformation can spread rapidly, it is of vital importance that science and education take center stage in public discourse. But, more fundamentally, we need to foster a collective mindset that is curious, critical, and always ready to learn and adapt. Only then can we hope to navigate the complex information landscape of the 21st century with clarity and wisdom.

9. Famous Cases Conspiracy theories have had a significant impact on the public perception of well-known historical events. Two of the most emblematic cases that have generated a vast amount of speculation and debate are the September 11, 2001 attacks and the assassination of President John F. Kennedy. These events, given their global resonance, have given rise to numerous theories that, in some cases, have become almost as popular as official explanations.

September 11 Attacks: On September 11, 2001, a series of coordinated terrorist attacks by al-Qaeda struck the United States. Four passenger planes were hijacked by terrorists: two were crashed into the World Trade Center's Twin Towers in New York, causing their collapse; a third hit the Pentagon in Arlington, Virginia; and the fourth, United Airlines Flight 93, crashed into a field in Pennsylvania after passengers attempted to regain control from the hijackers.

Almost immediately after these attacks, alternative theories began to circulate about what had really happened that day. Some of the theories suggested that the U.S. government was involved, or even that the attacks were an inside job to justify war in the Middle East. Other theories focused on alleged anomalies in the images of the collapsing towers, suggesting the use of controlled explosives. Despite these theories being widely debunked by experts and official investigations, they continue to persist for some.

Assassination of JFK: On November 22, 1963, President John F. Kennedy was assassinated in Dallas, Texas. Lee Harvey Oswald was arrested and charged with the murder but was killed two days later by Jack Ruby before he could be tried.

The assassination of JFK has given rise to a myriad of conspiracy theories, some of which have become part of popular culture. The theories vary widely, from involvement of the mafia, to the Cuban government, to the hypothesis that there were multiple gunmen on the day of the assassination. The Warren Commission, established to investigate the assassination, concluded that Oswald had acted alone. However, many people have questioned the Commission's findings, claiming that there were inconsistencies in the evidence or that there was a cover-up by high-ranking government officials.

In both cases, what is clear is that these traumatic events have left a gap in understanding. This gap, combined with distrust in institutions and the natural human tendency to seek patterns and meaning, has led to the birth and proliferation of alternative theories that attempt to explain these tragic events. Even though many of these theories have been debunked, their very existence demonstrates the profound human need to find order and understanding in the midst of chaos.

The very nature of conspiracy theories tends to flourish in times of uncertainty or after significant events. In this regard, September 11 and the JFK assassination represent fertile ground for speculation, given the immense emotional and political impact they had on society. Both events led to an intense debate about the ability of a fire, caused by the plane impacts, to bring down steel-framed buildings like the Twin Towers. Many conspiracy theory proponents pointed to videos and testimonies they believed indicated explosions at the base of the towers before their collapse. Additionally, the collapse of World Trade Center 7, a building near the Twin Towers that was not directly hit by a plane but still collapsed that day, has been the subject of much speculation. Some suggest that its collapse was due to controlled demolition.

Regarding JFK's assassination, conspiracy theories have not been limited to possible gunmen or their handlers. There have been speculations about the roles of the FBI and the CIA, inconsistencies in ballistics reports, and the analysis of Abraham Zapruder's famous film, which recorded the assassination in real time. The latter has become one of the most studied pieces of evidence in U.S. history, with analysts scrutinizing every frame for clues. Some conspiracy theorists argue that the trajectory of the bullets that struck Kennedy does not match Oswald's alleged firing position, suggesting the presence of a second shooter, positioned on the so-called "grassy knoll."

Other Historical Cases An additional element that fuels these theories is the death of key witnesses or figures connected to these events. In the context of JFK's assassination, there have been many premature or suspicious deaths, which have fueled the idea that there was a systematic attempt to cover up or eliminate individuals who could reveal the "truth."

Similarly, after September 11, there were rumors that some engineers or professionals who had expressed doubts about the official version of events had been threatened or had died under mysterious circumstances.

These events, in their complexity and tragedy, have become symbols in their own right. Their significance has transcended the facts themselves, becoming representations of people's doubts, fears, and distrust of institutions. And in this atmosphere, conspiracy theories have found fertile ground to grow, thrive, and, in some cases, deeply root themselves in the collective psyche.

The intricate labyrinth of conspiracy theories often approaches a kind of alternative historical narrative, where known and accepted details are reinterpreted or challenged, giving rise to new stories.

Another often-cited case in the pantheon of conspiracies is the 1969 Moon landing. Some argue that the landing never occurred and that it was an elaborate Hollywood production at the request of the U.S. government to win the "space race" against the Soviet Union. Arguments range from the absence of stars in photos taken by astronauts, to the flag waving in an atmosphere-less environment, to strange shadows in photographs. Even though these points have been refuted by experts in various fields, the theory still has many followers.

The 1947 Roswell incident is another pillar in the world of conspiracy theories. The official story tells of a weather balloon crash in Roswell, New Mexico. However, speculation that it was a genuine UFO and that the U.S. government had recovered alien bodies from the crash site has fueled decades of theories. Subsequent denials and government disclosures, rather than quelling speculation, often fueled it, creating a vicious cycle of mistrust and suspicion.

Even the death of Princess Diana in 1997 has given rise to a series of conspiracy theories. While the official version attributes her death to a tragic car accident, some theories suggest it was an orchestrated murder, perhaps to prevent an imminent marriage or due to potentially explosive revelations about the British royal family.

It is interesting to note that many conspiracy theories revolve around the perception of a hidden power or supra-national entity operating in the shadows. These entities are depicted as all-powerful and all-knowing groups capable of manipulating global events at will. This narrative, which may seem like the subject of a spy novel or a thriller movie, resonates with many people, likely because it offers a simple explanation for complex issues or traumatic events.

Some of these theories, over time, have become almost mythological, evolving into stories passed down from generation to generation. Like any myth or legend, the versions change, adapt, and evolve, but their essence remains: a story that challenges the official reality, questions the dominant narrative, and offers an alternative version of events.

In addition to the events and mysteries we have already discussed, there are numerous other historical and contemporary incidents that have been shrouded in the veil of conspiracy theories. These theories sometimes arise from a small grain of truth or from inexplicable events that do not have immediate or satisfying explanations.

The tragic death of Marilyn Monroe in 1962, officially classified as a probable suicide, has given rise to countless theories. Some argue that she was assassinated due to her alleged relationships with the Kennedy brothers and her potential threat to reveal state secrets. These speculations are fueled by elements such as her final phone calls and the mysterious circumstances of her death.

Another widely debated conspiracy theory concerns the secret society Skull and Bones, whose members are selected students from the prestigious Yale University. It is believed that many members of this secret society have held positions of great power in the United States, including presidents and industry leaders. Theories suggest that this secret society may have significant influence on global policies and operates behind the scenes to promote its interests.

The Mysterious Area 51, a military base located in Nevada, has long been the subject of speculation regarding UFOs and alien technology. While the U.S. government has acknowledged the base's existence, its specific activities remain highly classified. This has fueled theories suggesting that Area 51 is where experiments on aliens are conducted and where extraterrestrial technologies are studied.

The tragedy of Malaysia Airlines Flight MH370 in 2014, which disappeared while in flight and has not been found to this day, has also given rise to multiple conspiracy theories. These range from the idea that the plane was intentionally shot down or hijacked to being "abducted" by alien forces. The lack of definitive answers has fueled these speculations.

A recurring theme in many conspiracy theories is the concept of "hidden power." This is the idea that there are individuals or groups operating in the shadows, orchestrating global events according to a hidden agenda. These could include international bankers, global elites, or secretive organizations like the Bilderberg Group or Bohemian Grove.

The allure of these theories may lie in the human desire to find answers and meaning in events that appear chaotic or incomprehensible. In an increasingly complex world, where information is often fragmented and overwhelming, these theories offer an alternative narrative, a way to connect the dots and create a coherent story, even if not always based on verifiable facts.

Throughout history, conspiracy theories have been a way for humans to try to make sense of great mysteries, coincidences, or inexplicable events. The famous cases we have examined represent only a small part of the numerous theories circulating, but they are emblematic of the influence such theories can have on public opinion and the perception of events.

Starting with JFK's assassination, a critical moment in U.S. history, there have been ongoing debates and investigations into what really happened on that fateful day in Dallas. The impact of this theory, in particular, has led to deep distrust in the government and cast suspicion on multiple entities, from government organizations to individual individuals. JFK's assassination serves as a glaring example of how a conspiracy theory can infiltrate the collective psyche, causing many to doubt the official narratives presented by authorities.

On the other hand, the September 11 attacks have given rise to theories that have shaken entire communities and nations. Despite the many investigations and evidence contradicting many of these theories, their persistence demonstrates how highly impactful events, especially when shrouded in complexity and horror, can become fertile ground for speculation and suspicion.

In the context of these events and others less known, what emerges clearly is the power of alternative narratives. In an era where access to information is broader than ever, the ability to discern between concrete facts and speculation becomes crucial. Conspiracy theories can offer comfort to those who feel overwhelmed or powerless in the face of major global events, providing simple explanations for complex issues or presenting convenient scapegoats. However, they can also distort reality, fuel fear and hatred, and lead to decisions based on false premises.

In conclusion, while conspiracy theories have always been an immutable component of humanity's socio-cultural fabric, it is essential to approach them with critical thinking and an open mind. Recognizing the power and influence of such theories, both historical and contemporary, allows us to confront them with greater awareness and discernment, thereby safeguarding the truth and integrity of our understanding of the world.

10. Conspiracy Theories Related to Economic Power

- Rothschild, Rockefeller, and Others
- The Federal Reserve

Conspiracy Theories Related to Economic Power

The involvement of powerful families and central banking institutions in the realm of conspiracy theories has a long history. Individuals and families with vast financial interests often find themselves at the center of speculations regarding the hidden control and manipulation of the global economy and global policies. Let's delve into some of the most emblematic cases.

Rothschild, Rockefeller, and Others

Rothschild: Perhaps one of the most well-known and frequently cited families in the context of economic power-related conspiracy theories is the Rothschild family. Originating from Central Europe, this Jewish banking family expanded throughout Europe in the 18th and 19th centuries, establishing banking branches in major cities like London, Paris, Vienna, and Naples. Their financial influence and loans to various European governments have made them the subject of numerous theories, many of which are severely anti-Semitic. It is speculated that they secretly control global finances and orchestrate world events to their advantage.

Rockefeller: The Rockefeller family is another cornerstone of conspiracy theories related to economic power. Hailing from the United States, they amassed their fortune through oil, with John D. Rockefeller founding Standard Oil, which was later broken up into several companies, many of which are still energy industry giants today. It is believed that they have secretly influenced U.S. and global politics for decades through their vast wealth and philanthropic foundations.

The Federal Reserve

The Federal Reserve (often simply referred to as the "Fed") is the central bank of the United States and, due to its importance in the global economy, is frequently at the center of conspiracy theories. Founded in 1913, its role is to oversee U.S. monetary policy, stabilize prices, and maximize employment.

However, its establishment and operations have often been shrouded in mystery for the general public, leading to speculation. One of the most popular theories suggests that the Fed is not a legitimate part of the federal government but rather a private entity run by global banks for their own benefit. It is said that through the Fed, these banks exert hidden control over the global economy.

Other theories suggest that the Fed is responsible for creating economic bubbles and crises, with the goal of further consolidating power in the hands of a financial elite.

These theories, although widely debunked by historians and economists, persist. In many cases, they are fueled by misunderstandings or oversimplified views of the financial system and the secretive or complex nature of banking operations. Being critical and well-informed is crucial when approaching such theories, as the distortion of facts can have real and harmful repercussions on society and the economy.

Analyzing conspiracy theories related to economic power requires exploring the intricate web of families, institutions, and historical events that have often been used as pieces of a broader mosaic. Beyond Rothschild, Rockefeller, and the Federal Reserve, other recurring themes and controversial figures emerge.

Goldman Sachs and the "Big Banks": Goldman Sachs, along with other investment banks like JP Morgan and Morgan Stanley, is often at the center of conspiracy theories. It is claimed that these banks have disproportionate influence over Wall Street and government policies. Critics often point to the flow of personnel between Goldman and high-level government positions as evidence of hidden influence.

The "Seven Sisters" of Oil: In the mid-20th century, seven of the largest oil companies (Exxon, Mobil, Chevron, Gulf Oil, Texaco, BP, and Shell) dominated the global oil industry. These companies, known as the "Seven Sisters," have often been accused of manipulating prices, politics, and even global events to maintain their control over the oil market.

Soros and Financial Speculators: George Soros, a billionaire investor and philanthropist, has become a common target in conspiracy theories. Due to his speculative currency bets and support for various liberal causes through his Open Society Foundations, many accuse him of manipulating political and financial events.

The Bilderberg Group: Founded in 1954, the Bilderberg Group is an annual conference that brings together approximately 130-140 guests, including political leaders, finance experts, academics, and journalists. The private nature of these meetings has fueled speculation and theories that the group makes key decisions secretly influencing global geopolitics.

Bretton Woods and the Abandonment of the Gold Standard: In 1944, representatives from 44 nations gathered in Bretton Woods, New Hampshire, to establish a new international financial system. This system tied currencies to the U.S. dollar, which was in turn linked to gold. However, in 1971, the United States abandoned the gold standard, ushering in an era of fiat currencies. This transition has often been cited in conspiracy theories as a way for financial elites to control the global economy.

International Organizations: Institutions such as the International Monetary Fund (IMF) and the World Bank are often at the center of conspiracy theories. It is claimed that these organizations impose economic policies on developing countries, ensuring the supremacy of Western economic elites.

Economics of Shadows: It is believed that there exists an entire underground economy controlled by elite networks profiting from illegal markets, tax evasion, and other clandestine activities. This "shadow economy" is purportedly one of the primary sources of power for these groups.

It is essential to emphasize that while some of these elements are based on historical facts or real events, their interpretation or placement within a broader network of global control often relies on speculation or distortions.

Monopolies and Cartels: Throughout the 20th century, numerous industries have been dominated by cartels or monopolies. These groups, often with a strong concentration of power, have been accused of manipulating markets, prices, and even politics. One of the most well-known examples is the De Beers cartel, which controlled the production and distribution of diamonds worldwide for decades, significantly influencing prices.

Think Tanks and Lobbying: Think tanks such as the Council on Foreign Relations, the Trilateral Commission, and the American Enterprise Institute are often at the center of economic conspiracy theories. It is alleged that these organizations influence economic and political policies beyond their public mission statements, advocating for a world order dominated by financial elites.

Offshore and Tax Havens: Locations such as the Cayman Islands, Panama, and Switzerland are known as havens for global capital. The ability to transfer vast sums of money to these jurisdictions, often with little or no taxation, has been an obsession for those who believe that economic elites operate beyond the control of national governments.

Drafts of a Global Currency: At various times in recent history, there have been proposals to create a single form of global currency. Although these proposals have never gained traction, they have become a recurring topic in conspiracy theories, with the belief that a global currency could give economic elites unprecedented control over global finances.

Land and Resource Acquisitions in Africa: In recent decades, there has been significant land and resource acquisition in Africa by foreign entities. These "land grabs" have been criticized as a new form of colonialism, with foreign powers exploiting the continent's resources for their interests.

Free Trade Agreements: Agreements like NAFTA (North American Free Trade Agreement) or TTIP (Transatlantic Trade and Investment Partnership) are often the focus of conspiracy theories. It is argued that these agreements are designed not only to benefit large corporations but also to reduce national sovereignty, allowing economic elites to operate without restrictions.

Emerging Technologies and Control: With the rise of cryptocurrencies like Bitcoin, there have been theories suggesting that these new forms of money could be a way for economic elites to escape state control. Similarly, the adoption of technologies like artificial intelligence and automation might be seen as a means to further concentrate economic power.

Influence of Multinational Corporations:
Companies such as Apple, Amazon, and Google have
become global powers with financial resources
surpassing those of many countries. Their ability to
influence policies, markets, and even culture has been
the focus of many conspiracy theories, suggesting that
these companies may have a hidden agenda to
consolidate economic power.

Even in this context, it is crucial to distinguish between
legitimate concerns about the concentration of
economic power and unfounded conspiracy theories.
Many of the issues mentioned above have real bases
and are the subject of legitimate public debate, but
their interpretation within a conspiratorial framework
can distort reality and obscure real issues.

Markets and Manipulation: One of the most
discussed aspects of economic conspiracy theories
concerns the manipulation of financial markets. It is
alleged that institutions like the Federal Reserve, along
with other central banks, manipulate markets by
controlling stock market fluctuations, currencies, and
interest rates. These speculations stem from the
perception that central banks have absolute control
over the monetary system and can, through secretive
operations, cause economic crises or periods of
prosperity at their discretion.

Globalization and Control: The rise of
globalization has often been associated with the
expansion of the power of multinational corporations
and financial elites. This narrative suggests that while

globalization has brought economic benefits to some, it has also facilitated the ability of elites to consolidate power, often at the expense of workers and local governments. The creation of organizations like the World Trade Organization (WTO) and the International Monetary Fund (IMF) is often seen as part of this process, with these entities serving the interests of large corporations rather than ordinary people.

Tax Evasion and Wealth Accumulation: The concentration of wealth has become a growing concern globally. Conspiracy theories have highlighted the use of complex tax schemes, offshore funds, and intricate corporate structures as a means for economic elites to evade taxes and accumulate wealth. These concerns have been amplified by document revelations such as the Panama Papers and Paradise Papers, which exposed how the rich and powerful can exploit legal loopholes to protect their wealth.

Commodity Speculation: Some theories argue that large banks and investment funds manipulate the prices of commodities such as oil, gold, and food. This control, they claim, allows these entities to profit from both price surges and drops, often at the expense of consumers and producers.

Hidden Agendas of Economic Conferences: Events like the World Economic Forum in Davos or meetings of the Bilderberg Group are seen by some as places where economic elites secretly plan the future of the global economy. Although these events are often presented as open discussion forums, some conspiracy theorists argue that they are the epicenter of global economic decisions made away from the public eye.

Rise of Mega-Corporations: Mergers and acquisitions in various industries have led to the creation of mega-corporations with unprecedented powers. These entities, it is argued, have the ability to influence political decisions, control entire sectors of the economy, and manipulate public opinion through their media ownership.

Shadow Banking: "Shadow banking" refers to financial activities that occur outside the traditional banking system, such as hedge funds, private equity funds, and other investment vehicles. It is alleged that these entities operate outside of regulation and control, allowing economic elites to exploit the system for their gain.

The complexity of the global economic system provides fertile ground for speculation and distrust. While some of these theories contain grains of truth, it is essential to approach them with a critical spirit, distinguishing between legitimate concerns and unfounded theories.

The vast network of economic interconnections that weaves the modern world has always generated ample speculation. The structure and functions of financial institutions, especially those operating at high levels, such as the Federal Reserve or economically influential families like the Rothschilds and Rockefellers, are topics that are often shrouded in a cloud of complexity and secrecy. This intrinsic complexity, combined with the human tendency to seek patterns and meaning, has led to the birth and proliferation of numerous conspiracy theories.

In the economic context, these theories tend to focus on alleged secret maneuvers to control global resources, manipulate key economic events, and concentrate wealth in the hands of a select few. Speculation about the motivations and actions of these economic elites raises valid concerns about transparency, fairness, and accountability in the global financial system.

On the other hand, it is important to acknowledge that we live in an era of unprecedented access to information. While this can simplify the spread of conspiracy theories, it also provides the opportunity to fact-check and challenge such theories. The key is to promote critical education and encourage people to seek reliable sources, question their beliefs, and remain open to a variety of perspectives.

In conclusion, while conspiracy theories related to economic power raise important questions about the structure and transparency of our global financial system, it is essential to approach such theories with healthy skepticism. Examining claims, considering sources, and understanding the complexity of the economic world are essential steps in separating reality from fiction in the context of economic conspiracy theories.

Conspiracy and Religion: Religion, with its deep roots in human history and culture, has always played a central role in shaping collective and individual identity. It offers existential answers and provides moral guidance. However, like any powerful belief system, it can also be used - or rather, misused - as a means to manipulate the masses or justify controversial actions. In this context, many conspiracy theories have emerged over the centuries, connecting historical events, religious figures, and alleged secret agendas.

The Protocols of the Elders of Zion: The "Protocols of the Elders of Zion" is one of the most infamous and enduring examples of a conspiracy theory based on a falsehood. First published in the early 20th century, the document claims to reveal a secret Jewish plan to conquer the world. Despite being exposed as a forgery as early as the 1920s, the document has been used as justification for anti-Semitism and as propaganda against Jews in various parts of the world, including Tsarist Russia and Nazi Germany.

The Antichrist and the End Times: The figure of the Antichrist and prophecies related to the end times have roots in Christian theology. The Antichrist is traditionally seen as an evil figure who will emerge at the end of times, opposing Christ and deceiving many with false doctrines. This figure has been interpreted and reinterpreted in many ways throughout history, often being associated with political leaders or global events.

Many believers view biblical prophecies as literal warnings, while others interpret them symbolically. However, throughout history, some individuals or groups have exploited these beliefs to advance particular agendas, connecting current events to prophecies and claiming that the end times are imminent. This has often led to panic, millenarian movements, or destructive behavior.

In an era where information spreads rapidly and extensively through digital media, conspiracy theories related to religion can have a significant impact on people's perceptions and behavior. While religion can offer comfort and guidance, it is crucial to critically examine claims that seek to link religious dogma to conspiracy theories. This helps prevent the escalation of fear, hatred, and misinformation.

Conspiracy and religion, therefore, have an intertwined history, with religion often being used as a tool to justify or promote conspiracy beliefs. It is essential to recognize these intersections while also promoting a critical and reflective approach to religious dogma and conspiracy theories.

Conspiracy Theories in Islam: Taking Islam as an example, some conspiracy theories suggest that there is a Western plan to undermine or destroy Islam as a religion. These ideas are rooted in historical events such as the Crusades or modern colonization and have been fueled by contemporary policies and military interventions in majority-Muslim countries. Furthermore, the erroneous and unjust equation of

Islam with terrorism by some extremist factions has led to further speculation and distrust.

Evangelicals and the "World Conspiracy" Theory: In the United States, some conservative evangelical groups view the formation of a "world government" as a precursor to the rise of the Antichrist. Institutions like the United Nations or concepts like the "New World Order" are often interpreted through this lens. This view has been reinforced by popular book series like "Left Behind," which describes an apocalyptic future based on literal interpretations of biblical prophecies.

Messiahship and Salvific Figures: In many religious traditions, the expectation of a messiah or salvific figure is powerful. This anticipation can be easily manipulated or interpreted conspiratorially. When charismatic figures emerge claiming to have answers or solutions, they can be both revered as messianic figures and demonized as impostors or agents of evil. In both cases, emotional reactions and deep religious connections can fuel conspiracy theories.

Minor Religions and Cults: Minor religions or cults are often at the center of conspiracy theories. Sometimes, this is due to unconventional practices or beliefs. In other cases, it may stem from real instances of illicit or manipulative behavior by leaders. For example, the Church of Scientology has often been the subject of debates and controversies regarding its practices and its political and social influences.

It is also important to note how external sources can create or spread religious conspiracy theories to diminish or delegitimize a particular faith or religious group.

In conclusion, when religion and conspiracy intersect, the combination can be potent and potentially dangerous. Religious beliefs touch the hearts and souls of people, and when mixed with fear, distrust, and misinformation, they can lead to deep divisions, extreme behaviors, and, in some cases, violence.

Conspiracy and Religion: Final Reflections The connection between conspiracy and religion is complex, with roots that run deep in human history. At the heart of this interaction is a fundamental human need for understanding and order in a chaotic world.

1. **Historical Origins:** History shows us that conspiracy theories linked to religion have been present for millennia. From early Christianity, persecuted in the Roman Empire and convinced of the imminent end of the world, to witchcraft accusations in the Middle Ages, religion has often provided fertile ground for conspiracy theories.
2. **Need for Order:** Religion addresses fundamental existential questions about meaning, life, death, and the divine. When incomprehensible or tragic events occur, humans seek answers. If official or logically plausible explanations are unsatisfying, alternative explanations may be sought. Here, conspiracy

theories and religion can intertwine, offering an answer that, while unproven, can satisfy both logic and the soul.

3. **Social Impact:** Conspiracy theories related to religion can have serious social repercussions. They can fuel intolerance, discrimination, and, in some cases, justify violence. For example, anti-Semitism, often masked behind conspiracy theories like "The Protocols of the Elders of Zion," has had tragic consequences in history.

4. **Education and Knowledge:** A deep understanding of various religious traditions can help counter conspiracy theories. Understanding the beliefs and practices of a faith can demystify and reduce unfounded fears. Education can also provide the critical tools needed to analyze and debunk baseless conspiracy theories.

5. **Role of Religious Communities:** Religious communities have a responsibility to address conspiracy theories that emerge within them. Educating the faithful, promoting interfaith dialogue, and building bridges with the broader society can reduce the allure of conspiracy theories.

In conclusion, while conspiracy theories related to religion are a historical constant, their form and impact can vary. In an era of rapid information dissemination and increasing polarization, it is essential to address these ideas with a combination of education, dialogue, and understanding. Only through greater awareness and active engagement can we hope to reduce the influence of such theories and build more inclusive and tolerant societies.

Conspiracies and Popular Culture The influence of conspiracy theories extends beyond the realms of politics, religion, or economics; it has also deeply permeated popular culture. Films, music, and literature have reflected, and sometimes amplified, the conspiratorial beliefs of the public, giving them a broader platform and making such ideas accessible to a wider audience.

1. **Film:** Cinema, with its ability to visually engage the viewer, has often brought conspiracy theories to the forefront. Films like Oliver Stone's "JFK" have raised doubts about the circumstances of President Kenncdy's assassination, while movies like "The Da Vinci Code" have explored conspiracies related to the Church and the history of Christ. These films not only entertain but can also influence the public's perception of the reality of historical events.

2. **Music:** Music, especially in the rap and hip-hop genres, has often addressed themes of oppression, government control, and conspiracies. Artists like Tupac Shakur and Public Enemy have released songs that speak of government conspiracies, media control, and oppression. Even outside of hip-hop, artists like Bob Dylan and The Beatles have been the subject of conspiracy theories or have alluded to such ideas in their songs.

3. **Literature:** Literature provides a platform where conspiracy theories can be explored in depth, both as fact and fiction. Books like George Orwell's "1984" and Philip Roth's "The Plot Against America" present dystopian visions based on conspiracy ideas. While these are works of fiction, they have influenced the public's perception of real power dynamics and control in society. On the other hand, books like William Cooper's "Behold a Pale Horse" have attempted to expose alleged real conspiracies, influencing generations of conspiracy theorists.

This interplay between conspiracy and popular culture is a double-edged sword. On one hand, it can raise awareness of potential injustices and encourage healthy skepticism toward official narratives. On the other hand, it can also spread misinformation and perpetuate unfounded myths.

The power of popular culture lies in its ability to reach masses of people, shaping or influencing their opinions. Therefore, it is crucial for the public to maintain a critical approach to these representations, distinguishing between entertainment and facts. Yet, regardless of the degree of truth in conspiratorial representations in popular culture, they remain a testament to the profound influence that such ideas have on the fabric of modern society.

In the modern era, popular culture has assumed an increasingly important role in shaping public perception of historical events, figures, and ideologies.

This power to shape opinions is doubly significant when it comes to conspiracy theories, as the portrayal of such theories in the media can legitimize, disseminate, or diminish such beliefs.

Television Series: While films have the power to present a narrative within a span of two or three hours, television series can explore complex concepts over seasons, offering a depth that cinema often cannot afford. Series like "The X-Files" laid the foundation for a generation of skeptics, with its famous phrase "I want to believe" becoming a mantra for many. This series, in particular, explored numerous conspiracies, from the presence of aliens to the government's involvement in unspeakable secrets.

Video Games: In the world of video games, titles like the "Assassin's Creed" series have delved deeply into conspiracy theories, mixing historical facts with fiction to create gripping plots that span millennia of history and involve secret societies like the Templars and Assassins.

Podcasts and Documentaries: With the rise of digital media, podcasts and documentaries have become increasingly popular means to explore and discuss conspiracy theories. While some of these are purely speculative and entertaining, others strive to provide in-depth research, featuring interviews, evidence, and critical analysis.

Fashion and Branding: Even the world of fashion and branding is not immune to the influence of conspiracy theories. Logos, symbols, and slogans often draw from esoteric or conspiratorial themes to create an aura of mystery or attract a specific audience.

Art and Installations: Contemporary art often reflects society's concerns and obsessions. Installations, performances, and visual artworks have incorporated conspiratorial themes, stimulating dialogue and posing questions about power, truth, and reality.

Memes and Internet Culture: In an era dominated by social media, memes have become a powerful form of communication. Memes related to conspiracy theories can go viral in no time, spreading ideas at an unprecedented speed. However, this can also lead to rapid distortion of information, making it difficult to distinguish reality from fiction.

The pervasiveness of conspiracy theories in popular culture testifies to their resonance in the collective imagination. Whether it's a simple human curiosity, deep distrust in institutions, or a combination of both, it's clear that conspiracies will continue to find fertile ground in the public's mind and, consequently, in the cultural landscape.

Popular culture, in all its facets, has proven to be not only a reflection of society's beliefs and concerns but also a powerful lens through which these ideas can be amplified, distorted, or reimagined. When it comes to conspiracy theories and their interaction with popular culture, several key aspects come into play.

First and foremost, it is crucial to recognize that the way conspiracy theories are presented in the media directly impacts their perception. A positive or intriguing portrayal of a theory can legitimize it in the eyes of the public, even if it lacks concrete evidence. Conversely, a mocking or critical representation can diminish or ridicule the theory, making it less likely for the public to take it seriously.

Furthermore, with the birth and expansion of social media, the barriers between content producers and consumers have broken down. This has allowed anyone to contribute to cultural discourse, giving voice to opinions and theories that once may have been confined to the fringes. While this has resulted in an explosion of creativity and diversity in discourse, it has also opened the door to misinformation and manipulation.

Another critical aspect is how popular culture can be used as a vehicle to normalize or mainstream certain theories. For instance, when conspiratorial concepts are woven into the plots of popular films or TV series, they can become part of the collective consciousness, making it harder for people to distinguish between fact and fiction.

However, not all is negative. While popular culture can undoubtedly amplify or distort conspiracy theories, it can also serve as an educational tool. The representation of such theories in a critical context can stimulate discussion, prompting people to educate themselves and seek the truth. It can also serve as a warning about the dangers of misinformation and the importance of fact-checking.

In conclusion, while conspiracy theories have existed for centuries, their interaction with modern popular culture has made them more pervasive and powerful than ever. In this ever-evolving context, it becomes essential for the public to be informed, critical, and discerning when consuming content, recognizing the difference between entertainment and reality, and understanding the importance of seeking reliable and verified sources. Popular culture, in its role as a mirror of society, reminds us that while it may be tempting to succumb to the allure of mystery and secrecy, it is our duty as informed citizens to seek the truth beyond appearances.

Debunking Techniques Debunking, or dismantling false or misleading claims, is an essential component in countering conspiracy theories. Conspiracy theories, by their nature, are based on deep and often emotional beliefs, making challenging them a challenging yet essential task. Below are some techniques for effectively addressing such theories.

1. **Listen Carefully:** Before challenging a conspiracy theory, it's crucial to listen and try to understand the perspective of those who believe in it. Only by understanding their concerns and fears can you effectively address their beliefs.
2. **Use Credible Sources:** Conspiracy theories thrive in the absence of reliable information. When presenting a countermeasure, it's essential

to use credible and reputable sources. This includes academic organizations, recognized news agencies, and experts in the relevant field.

3. **Acknowledge Confirmation Bias:** Confirmation bias occurs when people seek or interpret information in a way that confirms their existing beliefs. It's important to highlight this bias when discussing conspiracy theories, as it can help people reflect on how and why they arrived at their conclusions.

4. **Employ Logic and Reasoning:** Many arguments in support of conspiracy theories rely on logical fallacies. Identify these fallacies and illustrate logical and rational alternatives.

5. **Provide Contradictory Evidence:** Presenting direct evidence that contradicts a conspiracy theory can be an effective way to challenge false beliefs. However, it's essential for this evidence to be concrete and easily verifiable.

6. **Pose Critical Questions:** Instead of directly presenting a countermeasure, sometimes it can be effective to ask questions that guide the person to think critically about their belief. For example, "How would you know if this theory were false?" or "Who would benefit from this conspiracy, and why?"

7. **Appeal to the Simplicity Heuristic:** The simplicity heuristic suggests that when there are multiple possible explanations, the simplest one (requiring the fewest assumptions) tends to be correct. Explain that, very often, simpler and more direct explanations are more likely than complex conspiracy plots.

8. **Be Patient and Compassionate:** Challenging conspiracy theories can be a lengthy and challenging process. Many people are deeply attached to their beliefs and may react with hostility or defensiveness. It's important to approach these discussions with patience and understanding, recognizing that changing a deep-seated belief takes time and effort.

Educational and Public Relations Approaches
In the era of post-truth, education plays a crucial role in providing individuals with the necessary tools to navigate a sea of often contradictory information. Media literacy and critical thinking become essential for discerning truth from falsehood.

Educate about the Difference Between Fact and Opinion: People need to be trained to recognize the difference between a fact, which is something verifiable, and an opinion, which is a personal belief or evaluation. This distinction, although seemingly simple, is often blurred in persuasive presentations.

Promote Scientific Thinking: Science, at its core, is a process of inquiry. It requires evidence, repeatability, and verification. Encouraging a scientific mindset helps people demand concrete evidence before accepting a claim as true.

Use Specialists for Conferences and Seminars: Inviting specialists from various fields to hold conferences and seminars on addressing and debunking conspiracy theories can be effective. These experts can share their experiences, provide concrete examples, and offer practical advice.

The Role of Online Platforms: Platforms like YouTube, Facebook, and Twitter have become key venues for the spread of conspiracy theories. However, these same platforms can be used for education. For example, educational videos that challenge conspiracy theories or explain the logic and science behind certain phenomena can reach a broad audience.

Create Discussion Groups: Establishing groups or forums where people can openly discuss their fears or concerns about specific conspiracy theories can be therapeutic. These spaces allow individuals to confront other viewpoints and subject their beliefs to critical examination in a safe and supportive environment.

Practical Examples and Case Studies: Often, examining a specific conspiracy theory can provide insights into how these myths form and spread. Analyzing and debunking specific conspiracy theories in detail can help people understand the general techniques used by conspiracy theorists.

School Involvement: Integrating media literacy and critical thinking into school curricula can provide the younger generations with tools to address conspiracy theories before they take root. This education may include practical exercises, guided discussions, and research projects.

When addressing conspiracy theories, it's essential to understand that these myths are often rooted in deep-seated fears and concerns. Challenging these myths requires sensitivity, understanding, and a holistic approach that considers both individual psychology and broader social dynamics.

Logic and Fallacies To understand and unravel conspiracy theories, having a solid understanding of logic and fallacies is fundamental. Many conspiracy theories are built on weak premises or unproven causal links. Here are some key concepts:

Post Hoc Fallacy: This fallacy suggests that if one event (B) follows another event (A), then A must have caused B. It's a common trap in conspiracy theories, where temporal coincidences are seen as proof of causality.

Slippery Slope Fallacy: The idea here is that one event will inevitably lead to another, often with negative outcomes. For example, the notion that a minor limitation on freedom of speech will lead to total oppression of freedom.

Confirmation Bias: This occurs when people seek and interpret information in a way that confirms their pre-existing beliefs, ignoring information that contradicts them.

Sophisticated False Equivalence: This happens when a comparison is made between two things that may seem similar on the surface but are vastly different in substance or context.

Recognizing Anecdotal Arguments: While personal stories can be powerful and engaging, they are not always indicative of a trend or broader truth. Conspiracy theories often rely on such anecdotes rather than concrete evidence.

The Role of Cognitive Biases: Every individual is subject to cognitive biases, systematic distortions in the way we perceive and interpret the world. For example, confirmation bias, where we tend to give more weight to information that confirms our pre-existing beliefs, or availability bias, where we tend to base our judgments on recently available information.

Using Effective Research Methodologies: To properly assess a conspiracy theory, it's essential to use robust research methodologies. This includes relying on reliable sources, critically analyzing information, and being able to distinguish between correlation and causality.

Questioning Plausibility: Some conspiracy theories would require an incredibly large number of people to keep the "secret." Asking whether it is practical or plausible for so many individuals to maintain a large-scale secret for an extended period can be an effective way to evaluate the truth of a theory.

Expertise and Competence: It's crucial to recognize and rely on experts in their respective fields. While any expert can make mistakes, a consensus among experts in a particular field is a strong indicator of the truth of a particular claim or theory.

The Importance of Self-Critique: Even as you debunk conspiracy theories, it's vital to be self-critical and open to the possibility that your own interpretations or understandings may be wrong. This open-mindedness not only strengthens your position but also promotes constructive dialogue with those who may believe in conspiracy theories.

Occam's Razor Principle One of the most useful guides in evaluating claims, especially those that appear complex or shrouded in intricate webs, is Occam's razor principle. It states that when presented with multiple possible explanations for a phenomenon, the simplest explanation (requiring the fewest assumptions) is usually correct. Many conspiracy theories are intricate and require the complicity of an incredibly large number of people, making their logic problematic and unlikely.

Constructive Criticism vs. Ridicule: A common trap many people fall into when confronted with conspiracy theories is to ridicule them. While tempting, this approach is rarely productive. Constructive criticism, based on facts and logically argued, is more effective. Approaching the discussion with an attitude of respect and understanding can also help create common ground and initiate constructive dialogue.

The Importance of Transparency and Accessibility of Information: In the digital age, there is an abundance of information. However, the quality of this information varies greatly. Promoting transparency and accessibility to reliable sources of information is crucial. Libraries, universities, and research institutions can play a crucial role in providing the public with tools and resources to discern accurate information from fake news or unfounded theories.

Theory vs. Hypothesis: It's essential to understand the difference between a theory and a hypothesis in a scientific context. In science, a theory is an idea that has been repeatedly tested and confirmed through observation and experimentation. A hypothesis, on the other hand, is an idea that has not yet been tested or verified. Many conspiracies are presented as "theories," but they have not undergone the rigorous scrutiny and testing required to be classified as such in a scientific context.

The Importance of Peer-Reviewed Literature: Another essential tool in debunking conspiracy theories is peer-reviewed literature. These are studies and research that have been critically reviewed by experts in the relevant field before publication. If a conspiracy theory is not supported by peer-reviewed evidence, it is likely lacking scientific foundation.

The Human Mind and Pattern Recognition: Our ability to recognize patterns is one of the reasons why Homo sapiens has been so successful as a species. However, this same ability can sometimes lead us to see connections and patterns where none exist, a phenomenon known as pareidolia. This predisposition can explain why some people are inclined to see hidden links and connections, thus fueling their belief in conspiracy theories.

Conclusion on Debunking Techniques:
Conspiracy theories, with their captivating narratives and seemingly intricate webs, have an undeniable allure and can significantly influence public opinion. That's why it is of paramount importance to possess the proper tools to evaluate these claims and distinguish them from solid, well-founded realities.

1. **The Rational Approach:** At the core of every debunking effort is rationality. Occam's razor principle, which suggests adopting the simplest explanation, is a fundamental guide. In practice, many conspiracy theories would require a vast network of people maintaining a perfect secret, which is highly unlikely.
2. **Respectful Communication:** A respectful and empathetic approach helps establish open dialogue. Ridiculing or belittling others' beliefs tends to reinforce those beliefs, whereas a constructive approach can lead to reflection and reconsideration.
3. **Information Transparency:** Ensuring that accurate and transparent sources are available and easily accessible can make a significant difference. Misinformation thrives when people don't know where to find reliable answers.
4. **Understanding Scientific Language:** Understanding the difference between terms like "theory" and "hypothesis" can help prevent

misunderstandings. Many misuse the term "theory," attributing it with more weight than it deserves.

5. **Importance of Peer-Reviewed Research:** Research that has been reviewed and accepted by experts in the field carries credibility far beyond that of blog posts or viral videos. Ensuring that claims are supported by peer-reviewed evidence is essential to assess their validity.

6. **Acknowledging Human Predisposition:** Our evolution has endowed us with a brain that seeks patterns and connections. This can be advantageous in many situations but can also lead us astray. Recognizing this predisposition can help question immediate conclusions and seek further evidence.

In summary, while conspiracy theories may seem captivating and at times even frightening, possessing the tools and knowledge to critically evaluate them is essential. Understanding, rationality, and an evidence-based approach are our best defenses against misinformation. In a world where false news can spread rapidly, each of us has a responsibility to seek the truth, challenge narratives, and promote understanding based on solid facts.

14. Conspiracies and Politics • Theories Related to Elections and Power. • Manipulation of Public Opinion.

Conspiracies and Politics

Politics, with its often nebulous nature and numerous actors, is fertile ground for conspiracy theories. These conspiratorial narratives can range from harmless speculations to serious distortions that influence public opinion and even political decisions.

Theories Related to Elections and Power

Elections, in particular, are events that garner significant public interest and can have profound repercussions on a nation's direction. Here are some common conspiracy theories related to elections:

1. **Electoral Fraud:** This is perhaps the most common conspiracy theory when it comes to elections. The idea is that there have been organized attempts to alter vote counts, manipulate voting machines, or intimidate specific segments of the electorate.
2. **Hidden Financiers:** The notion that politicians receive secret funding from powerful entities (corporations, foreign governments, oligarchs) to influence their policies and decisions is a recurring theme.
3. **"Puppet Candidates":** Some theories suggest that certain political candidates are merely

"puppets" controlled by hidden powers with the aim of advancing a conspiratorial agenda.

Manipulation of Public Opinion

The ability to influence public opinion is powerful and has significant political implications. Some conspiracy theories concerning manipulation include:

1. **Media Control:** The idea that major media outlets are controlled by a small group of powerful individuals who use them to shape public opinion according to their desires.
2. **Disinformation and "Fake News":** With the advent of social media, the spread of false or misleading news has become increasingly common. Many believe that there are organized efforts to spread disinformation in order to influence elections or other political decisions.
3. **Foreign Agents:** The idea that foreign powers (such as other governments or international entities) interfere in domestic politics, especially through propaganda or cyber warfare, is a growing concern.

The intersection of conspiracies and politics is as intricate as it is historical. Politics, often dominated by power dynamics and hidden interests, has always provided fertile ground for suspicion and alternative theories. While some conspiracies have historical roots, others are products of the modern era, fueled by the speed and reach of digital communication.

Instrumentalization of Conspiracies in Politics

Over the years, many leaders and political factions have used conspiracy theories as tools to advance their own agenda or to defame opponents. Accusing rivals of conspiracies or being part of hidden agendas can be an effective way to sow doubt among voters and undermine trust in the opposition. This tactic can also be used to divert attention from real issues or controversial government actions.

Conspiracies as Smokescreens

The very nature of politics—where decisions can have repercussions that affect entire nations or regions—means that much is at stake. Sometimes, conspiracy theories can be deliberate distractions, smokescreens created to divert attention from more serious issues or controversial government actions. Similarly, conspiracies can be used to sow confusion or suppress truthful information.

Global Conspiracies and Geopolitics

In addition to internal theories, many conspiracies focus on geopolitical events. Accusations of election interference, industrial espionage, or secret plans between nations are common themes. The perception of powerful global elites working behind the scenes to control world events is a constant in conspiratorial narratives.

The Risk of Echo Chambers

The digital age has amplified the speed and reach at which conspiracy theories spread. Platforms like Facebook, Twitter, and YouTube have created what is often called an "echo chamber," where individuals are primarily exposed to information that reinforces their existing beliefs, reducing exposure to contrasting viewpoints. This phenomenon has further polarized political opinions and strengthened conspiratorial beliefs.

The Transparency Dilemma

While transparency is considered one of the cornerstones of a democratic government, there are times when confidentiality is necessary for national security or diplomacy. This balance between transparency and secrecy can fuel conspiracy theories, with people suspecting that there is more to what is shown to the public.

Finally, it is crucial to recognize that while many conspiracy theories are unfounded, there are times when there are indeed conspiracies and deceptions at play. This reality further complicates the ability to discern truth from fiction in the political context.

The realm of political conspiracies extends beyond echo chambers or obvious manipulations; it branches into a myriad of subtopics and facets. Take, for example, history.

Era pre-digital: Conspiracies in the Last Century

Before the advent of the Internet, conspiracies primarily spread through pamphlets, radio, books, and word of mouth. This gave rise to legends such as the "New World Order" or theories about secret groups like the "Bilderberg." Some conspiracy theories, such as those related to the assassination of JFK, gained immense popularity and became topics of public debate.

Transnational Dynamics

Some conspiracy theories transcend national borders and acquire an international dimension. For example, the perception that there are "threads" connecting powerful elites in different countries, orchestrating global events such as wars, economic crises, or even pandemics.

Electoral System and Conspiracies

In many countries, elections are often at the center of numerous conspiracy theories. Accusations of electoral fraud, external interference, and manipulation of results are common themes in every election cycle. These perceptions can have profound repercussions on the legitimacy of governments and people's trust in the democratic process.

Conspiracies as a Tool of Control

We must not forget how some conspiracy theories have been and continue to be used by authoritarian regimes as tools of control. By creating an imaginary enemy or exaggerating an external threat, these regimes can justify repressive actions, civil liberties restrictions, and the persecution of minority groups.

The Issue of Media

While social media is often accused of amplifying conspiracy theories, we must not forget the role of traditional media. There have been cases where television broadcasters, newspapers, or radio have promoted or given space to conspiracy theories, contributing to their legitimization and dissemination.

Psychological and Social Aspects

From a psychological perspective, conspiracy theories often offer a simple explanation for complex or traumatic events. Moreover, believing in a conspiracy can make people feel part of an exclusive group that possesses a "hidden truth." This dynamic can strengthen community bonds but can also fuel divisions and hostility towards those who are "outside" that circle.

Economy and Power

In addition to political and social dimensions, the economy plays a crucial role in conspiracies. The perception that powerful economic elites control the fate of countries or the entire global economy is a recurring theme. This is related to conspiracies related to central banks, multinational conglomerates, and prominent financial figures.

In conclusion, the intersection of conspiracies and politics is a vast and complex topic that reflects the anxieties, fears, and tensions of society in every historical period.

Conspiracies and politics are two intrinsically intertwined realms in human history. The very nature of politics, characterized by power, ambitions, and conflicts of interest, provides fertile ground for the generation and dissemination of conspiracy theories. When we examine this relationship, it is crucial to consider some key dynamics:

The Nature of Politics: Politics, by its nature, is a struggle for power. During this struggle, information is often hidden, manipulated, or distorted to serve a specific agenda. This environment of secrecy and manipulation makes it easy for many to believe that dark forces are at work behind the scenes.

The Function of Conspiracy Theories: Conspiracies often serve as mechanisms of psychological defense. When people feel powerless in the face of major social or political changes, attributing these changes to hidden entities can provide a kind of reassuring explanation. Even if erroneous, the conspiracy theory can provide a sense of understanding and control.

Media and Manipulation: With the advent of social media and the explosion of digital information, spreading conspiracy theories has become easier than ever. However, traditional media outlets have also played a role in their propagation, especially when these theories served a political or economic agenda.

Long-term Implications: The growing distrust in institutions, partly fueled by conspiracy theories, has profound political repercussions. It can erode trust in democracy, hinder cooperation between countries, and weaken social cohesion. Conspiracy theories can influence political decisions, election campaigns, and even public policies.

In summary, while conspiracy theories may seem marginal or even ridiculous at first glance, they have a tangible and profound impact on politics and society as a whole. The challenge for journalists, educators, and political leaders is to address these theories critically, educate the public about the complexities of the world we live in, and promote critical and rational thinking. Only through education and engagement can we counter the tide of misinformation and restore trust in our democratic institutions.

15. The Danger of False Information

The Impact of Fake News

In the digital age, information travels at the speed of light. Social media, streaming platforms, blogs, and other means of communication have made knowledge more accessible than ever before. However, along with the expansion of these media, there has also been a surge in false information or "fake news." Their presence in our modern society poses a serious danger, not only to accurate information but also to the stability and cohesion of communities and nations.

The Impact of Fake News

1. **Erosion of Trust:** Fake news can quickly erode trust in institutions, media, science, and leaders. When people don't know what or who to believe, they can become cynical, apathetic, or, worse, vulnerable to further misinformation.

2. **Manipulation of Public Opinion:** Groups with specific agendas can use fake news to manipulate public opinion, thus influencing elections, referendums, and other political decisions.

3. **Social Polarization:** False information tends to create or reinforce information bubbles, where individuals are exposed only to information that reinforces their pre-existing beliefs, creating division and hostility between different groups.

4. **Risks to Public Health:** In the context of a health crisis, such as the COVID-19 pandemic, fake news related to treatments, vaccines, or safety measures can have fatal consequences.

Real Consequences of Unfounded Theories

1. **Violent Actions:** There have been a series of violent incidents triggered by unfounded conspiracy theories. For example, the conspiracy theorist behind Pizzagate led an armed man to a Washington, D.C. pizzeria, believing in an unfounded theory about an alleged pedophile network.

2. **Wrong Political Decisions:** Unfounded theories can influence political decisions, leading to ineffective or harmful public policies.

3. **Boycotts and Economic Damage:** Companies and individuals can suffer economic damage due to false information or conspiracy theories. Innocent businesses can be boycotted due to false accusations.

4. **Deterioration of International Relations:**
   Fake news can also influence diplomacy and
   relations between nations. False accusations or
   theories can create tensions or conflicts between
   countries.

False information, while not a new phenomenon, has
gained new resonance in the digital age. The ease with
which news can be created, modified, and shared has
changed the way information spreads. And, while there
are many reasons why people may intentionally share
misleading information, the consequences are almost
always harmful.

One crucial aspect of false information is the speed at
which it can go viral. Algorithms designed to increase
user engagement can often amplify sensational
content, regardless of its veracity. This means that a
single piece of fake news can reach millions of people
within hours.

The reasons why people rely on and share false
information vary. Some individuals are simply misled
by a well-crafted story. Others may find that a
particular piece of fake news confirms their pre-
existing beliefs or biases, making them less likely to
question it. Additionally, there is a psychological
tendency to believe information that evokes strong
emotions, such as fear, anger, or surprise.

Many organizations and individuals exploit these psychological dynamics to spread disinformation for their benefit. It can be state actors seeking to destabilize a rival country, groups aiming to promote a particular political agenda, or even individuals seeking to profit from the virality of sensational news.

Furthermore, false information is not limited to text. Deepfakes, which are digitally manipulated images or videos, are becoming increasingly sophisticated. These can be used to create clips showing people saying or doing things that never happened, making it even harder for the average observer to distinguish between reality and fiction.

But false information is not just about spreading false news. There are also intentional omissions, distortions, and misleading contextualizations. For example, a true statistic can be presented in a way that makes it deceptive, or a real event can be portrayed in a completely misleading context.

Another concerning aspect is the echo chamber effect of social media. People tend to interact with and follow individuals and information sources that share their own opinions and beliefs. This can create echo chambers where false information is repeated and amplified, further reinforcing erroneous beliefs.

This fertile environment for misinformation has led to new challenges for journalists, fact-checkers, and other organizations seeking to maintain the integrity of information. Attempts to correct false information can often feel like an uphill battle, especially when corrections do not receive the same visibility or level of engagement as the original fake news.

The Proliferation of False Information

The proliferation of false information also has a profound impact on the social fabric. The erosion of trust in traditional institutions such as the media, scientific organizations, and government authorities has been partly fueled by targeted disinformation campaigns. When people begin to doubt traditionally reliable sources, they become more vulnerable to alternative narratives, even if they are unfounded.

One of the most tangible examples of this phenomenon is the spread of health-related conspiracy theories. Misinformation about the causes of illnesses, treatments, and, more recently, vaccines, has had direct consequences on public health. Instances of measles, for example, have seen a resurgence in various parts of the world due to unfounded fears about vaccines, which have been fueled by false information amplified through social media.

But it's not only physical health that is at stake. The political landscape has also been deeply influenced by disinformation. False narratives concerning electoral processes, candidates, and political issues have distorted public discourse, further polarizing societies and undermining trust in the democratic process.

On the global stage, disinformation has become a tool of soft power. Some governments and organizations have created entire departments dedicated to information warfare, seeking to influence public opinion both domestically and internationally. This form of non-armed conflict can have lasting effects on international relations and the global perception of a nation or event.

The technology industry, for its part, finds itself in a unique and complicated position. On one hand, social media platforms are often criticized for not doing enough to combat the spread of false information. On the other hand, when they take actions to limit or remove misleading content, they are often accused of censorship or political bias.

Furthermore, the line between what is considered false information and what is simply an opinion or an alternative view of reality can be thin and subjective. This makes it even more challenging for technology platforms to establish clear and consistent content moderation policies.

Another complication is the ever-evolving nature of disinformation tactics. As new tools are developed to identify and combat disinformation, those spreading false information develop new methods to evade these measures. This arms race in the digital realm represents an ongoing challenge for those seeking to protect the integrity of information.

At the core of all this is a profound crisis of trust. In a world where truth seems increasingly fluid and subjective, many people feel lost and disoriented. This can lead to a sense of alienation and cynicism, where every piece of information is viewed with suspicion and where simple, reassuring narratives, even if blatantly false, can find fertile ground.

The phenomenon of false information and fake news is not just a technical or media challenge; it represents a fundamental threat to the very structure of our democratic societies. The ubiquitous nature of false information, empowered and amplified by the digital age, has generated a series of far-reaching implications and consequences.

First and foremost, trust is a cornerstone of any functioning society, and it is essential for the proper functioning of democratic institutions. When people can no longer trust sources of information or institutions that have traditionally provided guidance and truth, systemic fragility emerges. Without basic trust, social cohesion can begin to disintegrate, giving rise to divisions, polarization, and ultimately, instability.

Furthermore, false information fuels and amplifies political polarization. When different groups are exposed only to information that reinforces their pre-existing beliefs and view opposing opinions as not just wrong but also as threats or even harmful lies, it becomes nearly impossible to find common ground or promote constructive dialogue.

This climate of misinformation and distrust also has tangible repercussions. For example, decisions related to public health, such as the recent vaccine hesitancy, are directly influenced by the spread of erroneous information. These decisions can have deadly consequences, not only for those who choose not to vaccinate but also for surrounding communities.

On a Geopolitical Level, Disinformation as a Weapon

At a geopolitical level, disinformation has become a weapon. States and non-state actors use disinformation as a tool to destabilize enemies, influence elections, undermine trust in institutions, and promote their own agendas.

In the face of these challenges, it is essential to recognize the importance of media literacy and critical thinking. The population must be equipped with the necessary skills to distinguish reliable information from misleading information. Social media platforms and search engines have a responsibility to develop more effective mechanisms for identifying and countering disinformation. But beyond these technological efforts, there is a fundamental need to rebuild trust in institutions and promote open and honest dialogue in the public sphere.

In conclusion, while false information is not a new phenomenon, the current wave of disinformation empowered by the digital age represents an unprecedented challenge for modern societies. Its pervasiveness and profound ramifications require a multifaceted approach supported by individuals, institutions, governments, and technology platforms to ensure truth, transparency, and, above all, trust in our information ecosystem.

Case Study: Pandemic and Conspiracies

When the COVID-19 pandemic struck the world in 2019 and 2020, it created fertile ground for a myriad of conspiracy theories. This uncertain environment, coupled with fear and an initial lack of understanding of the virus, made people particularly vulnerable to false information.

COVID-19 Theories:

1. Origin of the Virus: One of the most persistent conspiracy theories was that the virus was deliberately created or released from a laboratory. Although extensive studies have indicated that the virus's origin is most likely natural and linked to bats, the debate over the exact origin continues.
2. 5G and COVID-19: There was a widely spread but unfounded theory that 5G towers would either spread the virus or exacerbate COVID-19 symptoms. This theory led to the destruction of several 5G towers in various countries.

3. Vaccines: With the development of COVID-19 vaccines, theories emerged suggesting that vaccines contained microchips to track the population or caused severe hidden side effects. Despite extensive clinical evidence of vaccine safety and efficacy, these theories hindered vaccination efforts in many regions.

Impact on Public Health:

1. Vaccine Hesitancy: Due to false information about vaccines, many people chose not to vaccinate, hindering global efforts to achieve herd immunity and prolonging the duration of the pandemic.
2. Ignored Precautionary Measures: Theories that downplayed the severity of the virus or promoted false cures led some people to disregard public health guidelines, such as mask-wearing, social distancing, and hygiene measures. This resulted in outbreaks and increased case numbers in many areas.
3. Strain on Healthcare Facilities: Distrust of official information and the adoption of unproven treatments often led to an overload of healthcare services, with patients seeking inappropriate treatments or avoiding treatment until their condition became critical.

The COVID-19 pandemic, with its global reach and implications for every aspect of daily life, raised questions and concerns for many people, creating fertile ground for conspiracy theories. The complexity of the pandemic, combined with a wide range of responses from governments and institutions, made some people suspicious and in search of "hidden truths."

Disinformation and Digital Platforms: While conspiracy theories have existed for a long time, the spread of such theories has been accelerated by digital platforms. The customization of news feeds based on algorithms has often created echo chambers where users are exposed to information that reinforces their existing beliefs, regardless of its accuracy. This echo chamber has further amplified conspiracy theories, making them visible to millions in a very short time.

Economic Impact: There has also been a significant amount of speculation and conspiracy theories regarding the economic impacts of the pandemic. Some have suggested that certain nations or companies deliberately allowed the virus to spread for economic gain. Others hypothesized that the entire pandemic was an orchestrated plan by global elites to consolidate economic power and control the masses through mechanisms such as tracking and lockdowns.

Data Manipulation: Another popular theme among conspiracists concerned the manipulation of COVID-19 data. While most global health organizations and research centers worked tirelessly to provide accurate data, there were moments when data was corrected or updated due to new information or unintentional errors. These adjustments, though normal in the world of science, were interpreted by some as evidence of a conspiracy to deceive the public.

Drugs and Treatments: The race to find effective treatments and a vaccine also led to the spread of many theories. Some claimed that home remedies or existing drugs could cure or prevent the virus, often based on anecdotes or preliminary research. When health organizations advised against using such treatments due to a lack of evidence, some saw this as an attempt to suppress a "cure" in favor of more expensive or profitable solutions.

International Organizations: Organizations like the World Health Organization (WHO) were at the center of many conspiracy theories. Their interaction with national governments, evolving recommendations based on emerging research, and critical decisions made during the pandemic were scrutinized and, in some cases, interpreted as part of hidden agendas.

These are just some of the numerous threads of conspiracy theories related to the COVID-19 pandemic. The environment of uncertainty and fear made many people more receptive to alternative explanations, often at the expense of understanding and informed action.

Public Reactions: One particularly interesting aspect during the COVID-19 pandemic has been the variety of public reactions to conspiracy theories. While many people embraced these theories as alternative explanations to those provided by mainstream media and health authorities, many others rejected these ideas as unfounded and potentially dangerous. This divide in perception often followed political, cultural, or regional lines, with some groups being more prone to believe in conspiracy theories than others.

Influencers and Celebrities: Some public figures, including celebrities, social media influencers, and even politicians, played a role in spreading or endorsing COVID-19-related conspiracy theories. Their platforms allowed these theories to reach a much wider audience and, in some cases, gain legitimacy in the eyes of many.

Bioengineering and Virus Origins: One of the most persistent theories concerned the origin of the virus. Some suggested that the virus was not of natural origin but rather the result of a failed bioengineering experiment or even intentionally released as a biological weapon. These claims, often based on misinterpretations or misleading scientific data, raised concerns and fear in many people.

Technological Challenges: The COVID-19 pandemic arrived at a time when technology plays a central role in our lives. Contact tracing apps, discussions about privacy and surveillance, and reliance on online platforms for news and information all contributed to a climate of mistrust. These technological challenges offered new opportunities for the spread of conspiracy theories but also raised legitimate questions about the role of big tech companies in content moderation and management.

Backlash Against the Scientific Community: While the international scientific community came together to seek answers and solutions to the pandemic, there was also a significant amount of distrust and skepticism from some quarters. This backlash manifested in various ways, from the rejection of scientific advice to suspicion of pharmaceutical companies, to opposition to lockdowns and other public health measures.

Global Narratives: The global scope of the pandemic also led to a variety of international narratives and interpretations. While some saw the crisis as evidence of global interdependence and the need for international cooperation, others interpreted it as a sign of the ineffectiveness of global institutions or as an opportunity to promote nationalist agendas.

All these facets of the COVID-19 pandemic and the associated conspiracy theories underscore the complexity of the situation and the need for critical thinking and accurate analysis in the information age.

Strumenti di Misinformazione: L'era digitale ha fornito una miriade di strumenti che possono essere utilizzati per diffondere disinformazione. Video manipolati, immagini fotoshoppate e post creati per apparire come fonti autentiche hanno inondato le piattaforme di social media. Questa sovrabbondanza di "prove" apparentemente autentiche ha reso molto più difficile per l'utente medio distinguere tra ciò che è reale e ciò che non lo è.

Teoria del Laboratorio di Wuhan: Una delle teorie più diffuse riguarda le origini del virus in un laboratorio di ricerca a Wuhan, in Cina. Sebbene la maggior parte degli scienziati abbia escluso questa possibilità, l'idea che il virus possa essere sfuggito accidentalmente o intenzionalmente da un laboratorio è stata alimentata da vari attori politici e media.

5G e COVID-19: Un altro esempio straordinario di teoria della cospirazione durante la pandemia è stata l'associazione tra le reti 5G e il COVID-19. Alcuni sostenevano che le onde radio emesse dalle torri 5G potessero trasmettere il virus o indebolire il sistema immunitario, rendendo le persone più suscettibili all'infezione. Questa teoria ha portato a atti di vandalismo contro le torri di telefonia in diverse parti del mondo.

Pharmaceutical Powers and Vaccines: As the race to develop a vaccine proceeded at a steady pace, many conspiracy theories began to circulate regarding the role of pharmaceutical companies. Some of these theories suggested that pharmaceutical companies had created the virus to sell the vaccine, while others questioned the efficacy and safety of vaccines, claiming they could cause long-term harm.

Social Changes and the World Order: Some conspiracy theories did not focus on the virus itself but rather on the social and political changes that followed the pandemic. It was argued that COVID-19 was a pretext to establish a new world order, limit civil liberties, or introduce more invasive surveillance systems.

Cultural Trends and Reactions: In various cultures, the pandemic awakened ancient fears and superstitions. In some areas, there were attacks against people considered responsible for spreading the virus or against ethnic or religious groups unfairly associated with COVID-19.

Country Comparisons: The management of the pandemic varied significantly from one country to another, giving rise to comparisons and speculations. While some countries were praised for their effective response, others were criticized. These differences led to theories about data manipulation, the reality of the severity of the pandemic, and the possible political motivations behind health decisions.

The vastness and complexity of conspiracy theories that emerged during the COVID-19 pandemic underscore the importance of clear, transparent, and evidence-based communication during global health crises. The spread of false information can not only hinder efforts to contain the disease but can also have serious consequences for social cohesion and trust in institutions.

The COVID-19 pandemic has been one of the most impactful and tumultuous events of the 21st century, influencing every aspect of society, from the economy to interpersonal relationships, from work organization to political dynamics. Amid this landscape of uncertainty and fear, the emergence and spread of conspiracy theories were almost inevitable, as humans tend to seek alternative explanations when faced with seemingly incomprehensible events.

The speed at which these theories spread was exacerbated by modern communication technologies. Social media, in particular, played a crucial role. They provided a platform for the rapid sharing and amplification of ideas, without the need for verification or filtering. This environment facilitated the proliferation of false or misleading information.

The theories that emerged regarding COVID-19 vary widely in nature and origin. Some arose from misinterpretations or misleading interpretations of scientific data, others from legitimate concerns distorted or exaggerated, and still others from pure speculation or malicious intent. The idea that the virus could be linked to 5G networks or that it could have been intentionally released from a laboratory are examples of groundless theories that gained global traction.

But these theories are not simply harmless speculations. They have had a tangible impact on public health and society at large. Vaccine hesitancy, for example, has been able to slow vaccination efforts and contribute to prolonging the crisis in some areas. Conspiracy theories have also influenced individual and collective behaviors, leading to incidents such as attacks on 5G towers or episodes of discrimination and violence against certain ethnic or national groups.

In conclusion, the phenomenon of conspiracy theories related to the COVID-19 pandemic highlights the complex interplay between information, perception, and behavior in modern society. It demonstrates the need for clear, accurate, and timely communication by authorities and healthcare organizations, but it also underscores the importance of critical education and media literacy among the general public. In an increasingly interconnected and digitized world, the ability to discern reliable information from misleading or false information becomes an essential skill to ensure well-being and social cohesion.

Conspiracy theories, if left unchecked, can have serious consequences, from undermining trust in institutions to driving socially harmful or even violent behaviors. For this reason, it is essential to develop and implement effective strategies to counter the spread and adherence to these theories. Here is an overview of counter-strategies focused on education, awareness, and media responsibility.

Education and Awareness

1. Critical Thinking: Education should have a strong focus on developing critical thinking. Students should be equipped with the tools needed to analyze and evaluate information objectively and logically. Through exercises, debates, and case studies, they can learn to recognize biases, falsehoods, and fallacious reasoning.
2. Media Literacy: In an era dominated by digital media, the ability to navigate, understand, and critically evaluate media content is crucial. Students should be educated about how search engines work, the mechanisms of social media algorithms, and how information bubbles form.
3. History of Conspiracy Theories: Knowing past conspiracy theories can help people recognize the patterns and tactics used by modern conspiracy propagators. This historical understanding can also serve as a deterrent, showing the potential harmful consequences of false beliefs.

Media Responsibility

1. **Ethical Journalism Standards:** It is essential for the media to maintain and promote ethical journalism standards. This includes accurate fact-checking, avoiding sensational headlines, and citing reliable sources.
2. **Combating Fake News:** Platforms like Facebook, Twitter, and Google have a responsibility to identify and reduce the spread of false or misleading news. This can be achieved through the use of advanced algorithms, fact-checking, and user reporting.
3. **Promoting Expert Voices:** In times of crisis or confusion, the media should prioritize the voices of experts. For example, during a pandemic, the opinions of virologists, epidemiologists, and healthcare professionals should take precedence.
4. **Open Dialogue and Transparency:** The media should encourage open dialogue and transparency, allowing for discussion and constructive criticism. This helps build trust and reduces the space for speculative theories.

Strategies to counter conspiracy theories are essential in modern society, and the key to their effectiveness lies in a holistic approach involving various spheres of public life.

Interpersonal Dialogue The power of face-to-face dialogue cannot be underestimated. Direct conversations, conducted with empathy and active listening, can help challenge mistaken beliefs. Here are some techniques that can be used:

- **Empathy and Active Listening:** When people feel heard and understood, they are more inclined to open their minds to new information. Avoid discussing aggressively or derisively, as this can lead to further resistance.
- **Providing Concrete Examples:** Tangible examples and personal stories can be more persuasive than simple statistics or facts.
- **Acknowledging Partial Truths:** Some conspiracy theories may contain grains of truth. Recognizing these aspects can help build a bridge to a broader and more accurate understanding.

Public Awareness Campaigns Public awareness campaigns can target a broad audience, using various channels to reach people of all ages and social backgrounds.

- **Testimonials:** Presenting stories of people who once believed in conspiracy theories but later changed their minds can offer a powerful and persuasive perspective.
- **Infographics and Visual Content:** People often respond better to visual information than text. Clear and well-designed infographics can break down complex topics into easily digestible formats.

Collaboration with Online Platforms Online platforms, especially social media, are fertile ground for the spread of conspiracy theories. However, they can also be used as tools to combat them.

- **Webinars and Training:** Organizing online training sessions to educate the public on how to recognize and counter false information.
- **Collaborating with Influencers:** Influencers can have a significant impact on the opinions of their followers. Working with them to promote accurate information can expand the reach of education.

Legislative Approaches The legislative approach is delicate as it interacts with freedom of expression. However, there are measures that can be taken:

- **Defamation Laws:** Strengthening defamation laws can discourage the spread of false information that can harm individuals or organizations.
- **Platform Responsibility:** Online platforms can be encouraged or obligated to take measures against the dissemination of disinformation.

The challenge of conspiracy theories is vast and ever-evolving, requiring an equally dynamic and multidimensional response. Through a combination of education, communication, collaboration, and, if necessary, legislative interventions, it is possible to build a more informed and resilient society.

Combating conspiracy theories is a complex undertaking that requires coordinated action on multiple fronts. While the expansion of the digital age has amplified the reach and speed at which these theories can spread, it has also provided new tools and methods to combat them. The key to effectively addressing this phenomenon lies in adopting a holistic strategy that integrates psychological, educational, media, and legislative approaches.

Education and awareness are the first line of defense. Teaching people to think critically, evaluate sources, and recognize signs of false information can prevent these ideas from taking hold in the first place. However, education does not stop in the classroom. Public awareness campaigns, supported by government organizations, NGOs, and other groups, can reach a broader audience, providing accurate information and directly challenging false narratives.

The media plays a crucial role in this ecosystem. They have a responsibility not only to provide accurate information but also to actively correct false narratives. Collaboration with online platforms, in particular, is essential given their role in the spread of conspiracy theories. Social media platforms can adopt algorithms to reduce the visibility of deceptive content and promote accurate information. Additionally, they can collaborate with external experts to fact-check content and provide context where necessary.

The **legislative aspect** cannot be ignored. While freedom of expression is a fundamental right, there are limits, especially when misinformation can cause tangible harm. Laws can be shaped to balance these rights with the need to protect the public.

In conclusion, countering conspiracy theories requires a multi-faceted approach that considers the complexity of the issue. There is no one-size-fits-all solution, but with combined efforts from educators, media, online platforms, and lawmakers, collective resistance against the tide of misinformation can be built. The key is collaborative action: every segment of society has a role to play in ensuring that the truth prevails.

19. Conclusions • Lessons Learned • The Future of Conspiracy Theories

Conclusions Conspiracy theories are not a new phenomenon, but their scope and impact have exponentially increased with the advent of digital media. Their existence and persistence result from a complex interplay of psychological, social, political, and technological factors. Through in-depth analysis of the various aspects of this phenomenon, we can draw some important lessons and reflect on the future of conspiracy theories.

Lessons Learned:

1. **Deep Understanding:** To effectively combat conspiracy theories, it is essential to understand their roots and motivations. Fear, insecurity, the need to find an enemy, or a simple explanation for complex problems are just some of the psychological reasons behind such beliefs.

2. **The Importance of Critical Education:** Teaching people to think critically, evaluate sources, and distinguish between accurate information and misinformation is crucial. Education goes beyond the school environment and must permeate society at all levels.

3. **Media Responsibility:** The media plays a crucial role in informing the public. They must be aware of the impact they can have and actively work to provide accurate and balanced information.

The Future of Conspiracy Theories:

1. **Persistence and Adaptability:** Although conspiracy theories are as old as humanity itself, they constantly adapt to the times. With the emergence of new technologies and the evolution of society, new conspiracy theories will inevitably emerge, adapting to the current context.

2. **Increased Interconnectivity, Greater Spread:** The interconnectedness offered by globalization and technology means that theories can spread more rapidly than ever before. This poses a significant challenge to debunking and correction efforts.

3. **Potential for Greater Resilience:** With increased awareness and educational efforts, there is also a greater opportunity to build a society more resilient to false narratives. Critical education and the promotion of truth will become increasingly essential in shaping the future.

In conclusion, conspiracy theories will remain a persistent part of the social fabric, but with deep understanding, effective education, and media responsibility, society can be better equipped to address and mitigate their impact. The key will be maintaining a collective commitment to truth, rationality, and shared humanity.

Conclusion: Conspiracy Theories - An In-Depth Overview

Conspiracy theories are an integral part of human culture and history. This book has sought to provide a comprehensive analysis of the phenomenon, exploring both its origins and contemporary manifestations. We have journeyed through:

1. **Historical Introduction:** Where conspiracies originate and how they have evolved over time.

2. **Means of Dissemination:** The evolution of traditional media and the rise of social media as vehicles of dissemination.

3. **Popular Theories:** From the influence of the Illuminati to mysterious UFO theories.

4. **Psychological Factors:** The innate human need to find meaning, order, and sometimes an enemy.

5. **Social Impact:** Conspiracies and their repercussions on trust in the system and political decisions.

6. **Science and Education:** The struggle between evidence-supported facts and entrenched beliefs.

7. **Famous Case Studies:** Historical events that have fueled numerous conspiracy theories.

8. **Economy and Power:** How some families and organizations have become the focus of many conspiracies.

9. **Religion:** Conspiracies intertwining with religious beliefs.

10. **Popular Culture:** The representation of conspiracies in film, music, and literature.

11. **Debunking Techniques:** Tools and methods for debunking unfounded theories.

12. **Politics:** How conspiracies can influence public opinion and political decisions.

13. **The Danger of Misinformation:** The era of fake news and its consequences.

14. **Case Study - Pandemic:** The emergence of conspiracy theories during global health crises.

15. **Counter Strategies:** The importance of education and the role of media in addressing misinformation.

16. **Conclusions and Reflections:** Lessons learned and thoughts on the future of conspiracy theories.

17. **Bibliography and Sources:** A guide to the resources used and recommended.

Guides and Useful Resources: For those wishing to delve deeper, here are some websites and guides that may be helpful:

1. **Skeptical Inquirer** (www.csicop.org/si): A magazine dedicated to promoting science and reason, regularly addressing conspiracy theories.

2. **FactCheck.org:** A resource dedicated to fact-checking and debunking false or misleading information.

3. **Snopes** (www.snopes.com): One of the earliest fact-checking websites, focused on verifying urban legends, rumors, and conspiracy theories.

4. **The Conspiracy Theory Handbook:** A guide providing tools to understand and challenge conspiracy theories.

5. **Media Education Foundation** (www.mediaed.org): A resource dedicated to critical media analysis.

Always remember to approach any topic with an open but critical mind, evaluating sources and reflecting on information before drawing conclusions. In an era where information is at our fingertips, learning to discern between fact and fiction is essential.